MW00780793

Firestorm!

Firestorm!

THE STORY OF THE 1991

EAST BAY FIRE IN BERKELEY

by Margaret Sullivan

 CITY OF BERKELEY, CALIFORNIA

Copyright © 1993 by the City of Berkeley, California. All rights reserved. No part of this book may be reproduced in any form without permission in writing from the publisher, except by a reviewer who may quote brief passages in a review.

United States Constitution, First Amendment: Congress shall make no law respecting an establishment of religion, or prohibiting the free exercise thereof; or abridging the freedom of speech, or of the press; or the right of the people peaceably to assemble, and to petition the Government for a redress of grievances.

Design and production coordination: Zipporah W. Collins
Copyediting: Alice H. Klein
Word processing: Diane Weston
Typesetting: Stanton Publication Services
Proofreading: Judy Bess, Fran Taylor
Printing and binding: Data Reproductions Corporation

Printed on acid-free paper
Manufactured in the United States of America

For information or additional copies, call or write to:
Office of the City
  Manager
City of Berkeley
2180 Milvia Street
Berkeley, California
  94704
510-644-6580

Cataloging-in-Publication Data Supplied by the Berkeley Public Library
Sullivan, Margaret.
  Firestorm! : the story of the 1991 East Bay fire in Berkeley / by Margaret Sullivan.
    p. cm.
  ISBN 0-9638265-0-6
  1. Fires—California—Berkeley. 2. Fires—California—Oakland. 3. Wildfires—California—Oakland. I. Title.
SD421.32.C2   1993
363.3492—dc20   93–073253
                                                              CIP

5 4 3 2 1

Contents

ACKNOWLEDGMENTS

As Berkeley's Fire Chief Gary L. Cates and then–City Manager Michael F. Brown drove through the blazing fire zone on October 20, 1991, they realized they were in the midst of what was to be one of the major episodes in Berkeley's history. Seeing the devastation of scores of houses and of entire neighborhoods, it occurred to them that a written account was needed to record the human story and events. They conceived the idea of a book to be written as a piece of history and as a public service.

This book is intended as a commemoration of that day in Berkeley. It is a record of contemporary history set down while the events were still "warm." The hope is that as the events recede from current memory, here they will continue to resonate. In giving voice to the Berkeley residents who found themselves in the fire's path and to the Berkeley firefighters who battled the blaze, the book depicts selected frames of the bigger picture of the entire East Bay fire. Although the fire burned an even greater swath through Oakland, the focus here is on Berkeley. We believe the Berkeley stories contain common and universal truths, not only for those who lived through the fire, but for every reader concerned with fire and interested in the drama of human nature confronted by a natural disaster.

In gathering the stories of evacuation and dislocation, I encountered people who were still feeling vulnerable from their experience in the fire. Their openness in speaking to me was touching. As one fire area resident said, "There is a beauty in dealing with this stuff." I thank each and every one of the fire survivors (we learned not to call them "victims") whom I interviewed for their willingness to share their personal stories and reflections. Sometimes we met in a group, and in sharing experiences with each other, these people found that a healing process was taking place.

Thanks to the Berkeley Fire Department for its great enthusiasm and support for this project. Fire Chief Cates made sure that all department records on the fire and all personnel were available to me. He did not flinch from the hard or controversial issues, and he encouraged me to explore them fully. My gratitude to the Berkeley firefighters is immeasurable. I received complete cooperation and good will from every person I interviewed. As my understanding of the fire developed, I returned to some of the same firefighters time after time for further insights and clarification and was always greeted enthusiastically and generously. Captain David Orth (now assistant chief), Assistant Chief Paul Burastero, and Fire Marshal Gary Bard (now deputy chief) all gave me invaluable assistance over the duration of the project in learning the details and technical aspects of the East Bay fire and of firefighting in general. Thanks too to the Fire Prevention staff, who gave me a place to work in their office and made me feel welcome.

While the book profiles certain specific firefighters who battled the firestorm, this focus is not meant to imply that the efforts and adventures of the others were not just as harrowing or heroic. For dramatic purposes I chose to let the few stand for all, rather than to give an encyclopedic account of every activity. This account is dedicated to the efforts of each Berkeley firefighter who served that day, on the fire front or behind the scenes managing logistics or covering the rest of the city. And it is dedicated to every man and woman in the Berkeley Fire Department. They now are part of history.

This story was written in the spirit of healing and reconciliation. The fire tore asunder the comfortable fabric of daily life: neighborhood, a sense of security in one's home, confidence in public safety systems. It strained and in some cases changed relations between family members and spouses. Firefighters risked their lives, but were stunned that they could not always hold the fire line. They wondered why the community did not universally acknowledge their efforts. Burned-out residents felt anger and frustration because their houses were not saved.

The public perception of the plight of the people who lost their homes, whose neighborhood was one of the more affluent in Berkeley, sometimes came up short on compassion. These Alvarado and Vicente road homeowners were viewed as having the monetary resources to cushion them from the effects of the tragedy. Their situation as newly "homeless" was not taken seriously. But while they were able to recoup the dollar value of their losses, the homeowners were not immune from trauma. It was observed more than once, including by these homeowners themselves, that they were people accustomed to having control over every aspect of their lives, people in charge. The fire stripped them of control. From the fire emerged the common human denominators of panic, bravery, loss, anxiety, disorientation, healing, and hope.

The book is offered also in the spirit of public service. It is presented as a "time capsule for the future." It sounds the warning about the peril of ignoring fire safety in areas adjacent to the fire-prone hills. Residential developments throughout California and the West that lie on the edge of dry, brushy, open space are at risk from the "wildland-urban fire." Wildland fires have struck the Berkeley-Oakland hills repeatedly over the decades, burning down houses, yet building practices and fire prevention measures have been slow to change. Or if they have changed, improvements have sometimes been short-lived. We hope that through this book the awareness of the need to maintain vigilance will be kept alive.

Thanks go to the donors whose contributions helped make this publishing effort a reality: the East Bay Community Foundation, the Berkeley Fire-Fighters Association, the Nature Company, and Pacific Gas & Electric.

Thanks to the photographers: Harold Adler, Lieutenant John Anderson of the Berkeley Fire Department, Ron Delany, Tom Levy of the *San Francisco Chronicle,* Kendra Luck, Michael Mustacchi, Jane Scherr, and Wesley Wong of the *Contra Costa Times*. Their sensitive and timely photographs of the fire and its aftermath capture the drama and enhance the story. Thanks too to the California Office of Emergency Services for its map of the firespread; to Norma Hennessey, graphic designer for the city of Berkeley, who adapted that map for use in this book; and to Thomas Bros. Maps for use of its map. We are also grateful to the citizens—Lu Arenson, Phil Gale, Jessie and Jeff Grote, and Debbie and Michael Lesser—who found photos in their family archives to lend us.

Finally, I want to acknowledge my debt of gratitude to the numerous city employees, private citizens, and friends who provided me invaluable guidance and suggestions throughout this project.

Margaret Sullivan
Berkeley, California

Introduction

The East Bay fire of October 1991 that roared out of the dry, northern California hills on the eastern side of San Francisco Bay has taken its place in the records as the most destructive wildland-urban fire in U.S. history. More than three thousand dwellings burned and twenty-five people died. Hundreds fled in the path of the fire, which burned for nearly three days over eighteen hundred acres before it was declared under control. What had started the day before as a small grass fire in the tinder-dry Oakland hills was reignited on the morning of October 20 from still-smoldering hot spots and whipped into conflagration proportions by strong, hot winds gusting to sixty miles an hour. Firefighters attempting to contain the fire as it leapt out of control that morning reported that the flames jumped 100 yards in ten seconds. Fierce, erratic winds fanned the grass fire into a firestorm. The winds carried flaming pieces of tree branches like torches to spread the fire to an ever-widening range. Hilly terrain concealed the magnitude of the fire until flames burst over one hill and raced down into the next canyon. In the face of a fire that didn't "play by the rules," new firefighting strategies had to be devised on the spot, and some painful decisions had to be made.

Within one hour 790 homes were lost. The blaze raced from treetops to rooftops, crossed two major freeways, and raged across city boundaries between Oakland and Berkeley, consuming entire neighborhoods and leaving a charred path of devastation in both cities. By the end of the fire 3,354 single-family homes and 456 apartment units had been destroyed.

The fire transformed tree-sheltered streets into a stark wasteland that in some places stretched as far as the eye could see. In the space of hours, neighborhoods established sixty, seventy, and eighty years ago vanished. Newer houses, nestled into canyons or perched on hillsides, were simply swept away when the unstoppable fire raged through.

What was left was an incinerated landscape devoid of familiar forms. The tree-covered hillsides were suddenly bare of protective foliage. Blackened trees stood as if stunned by the burn force they had endured. Exposed foundation walls formed patterns against the hills, traces of the houses that were. Only chimneys remained upright on the house plots, their presence awkward and mournful. The rest seemed to have been vaporized by a bomb blast, so little was left besides ash.

The toll on the fire survivors was staggering. Losses reached $1.5 billion, but aside from the material cost, the trauma of the fire exacted a human toll that is ongoing and hard to calculate. The sudden loss of home, with the sense of place, order, routine, and personal history it represents, constituted a kind of psychic amputation. The survivors' reactions ranged from bitterness and anger to dislocation and grief to exhilaration at the opportunities for new beginnings.

The story of the men and women who fought the fire is one of bravery and personal risk against life-threatening odds. One firefighter and one police officer died, and many were injured. Part of the story is that of courageous citizen volunteers who worked side by side with the firefighters, dragging hoses and beating back the fire front.

Facing page: The fire transformed tree-sheltered streets into a stark wasteland almost devoid of familiar forms. Photo © 1991 Harold Adler.

The fire departments attacked the conflagration with battlelike strategies and discipline. Likewise, the cities involved responded to the emergency like communities under siege. City officials huddled in "emergency operations centers" around the clock, deploying relief and clean-up crews and tracking the progress of the fire. Gas and electric workers arrived to cut off utilities as exposed gas jets flared and power poles went up in flames and crashed to the

ground, spreading live electrical lines. Hospitals were on yellow and then red alert, extending shifts to treat the burned and smoke-injured. The fire made a high number of local doctors and hospital staff homeless, even as they were treating others. The news media worked the front lines, sometimes battling their way through the confusion of conflicting fire department and police restrictions to get to the scene. Their recording of the tragedy and heroism was often an act of heroism in itself.

In the aftermath of the fire, criticism raged. Fire department, zoning, building, and wildland management practices all came under attack. Shake roofs, narrow streets, and the flammable eucalyptus tree were identified as culprits. Nervous residents demanded assurances that they would be protected from any future major fire. Officials seized the opportunity to call for tougher building standards and brush clearance enforcement. Fire departments instigated more formalized mutual response procedures between cities, including critical fire weather warnings. When they examined their radio communications systems and found them lacking, they drew up plans for improvements.

While the fire provided the impetus for preventative changes, the follow-through was another matter. Many of the recommended measures required the kind of commitment to public spending that has diminished in the last decade, as local municipalities have been left with less and less of the federal and state tax dollar. Public officials worried that as the experience of the fire faded so would the resolve to change things. Vested interests bumped up against one another. Homeowners racing to rebuild resented being saddled with new, restrictive fire prevention requirements, complaining that they were being treated as "guinea pigs." Local governments chose not to make radical changes in building-density requirements and street widths, settling for greater space between houses and for parking restrictions to keep narrow streets clear. The public was told that the cost of increased fire preparedness and prevention would be higher taxes or the risk of another uncontrolled conflagration in the future.

As each new fire season approaches, the questions remain: Will people keep building in inaccessible places? Will they use firesafe materials?

Will they plant fire-retardant vegetation and keep brush cleared? Will cities allow dense developments to be carved into hillsides? Will urban fire departments learn wildland firefighting techniques? Will critical fire weather be factored into fire department readiness? Will city governments spend what is necessary to coordinate emergency response—from training dispatchers to establishing protocols with surrounding cities?

How safe is safe in the dry, brushy hill areas of the West? Is it possible to manage the wildland-urban intermix? Can human beings assume their security in the midst of an indifferent nature? Are wildfires inevitable? If so, is it crazy to build houses on the edge of undeveloped wildlands?

Living on the Edge

The California Ethos

California, the golden state, was invented in the imagination before it was settled. From the enticement of instant wealth in the gold rush of 1849, to the promise of eternal sunshine in an Eden of orange groves as offered by the Southern Pacific Railroad's extravagant travel posters for the transcontinental trip, to the fantasy of the motion picture set, California has held out the possibility of dreams coming true. On the edge of the continent, California was the destination of those looking for a new beginning. In such a paradise even the self could be created anew.

Like the frontier ideal of the rugged loner pitted against the elements, the California ethos is grounded in a sense of the individual. Juxtaposed against the harshness of nature, the individual flirts with its risks, claims them as a defining element in the frontier personality, and also denies them. Because the old frontier is gone, the individual searching for self-definition must invent new ones. The creative act of self-expression was always the real frontier in California, and it remains the last.

In no other state is an individual more identified with the home than in California. How and where one lives defines one's taste, status, and values. The appeal of a house in a natural setting has as much to do with a desire for escape, privacy, and exclusivity as with Thoreauvian yearnings. The house is the California dream made manifest.

Living in places no one else can reach bespeaks a privilege that is not so much bestowed as taken. That is, after all, how the West was won. Living in the margins between civilization and wilderness produces the illusion of reconciliation between ease and danger—a sort of movie set existence. Coyotes, drought, wildfire, flash floods, mudslides, and earthquakes are regular occurrences for Californians dwelling on the edge of wildlands—but they are intermittent events. The moment of highest concern is always right after a disaster; then the urgency fades and the denial sets in. For newcomers with no memory of the last fire or flood the next one is especially a shock. For the Californians who live in severely graded subdivisions the wildland context and consequences are easily overlooked. Highways and streets, the concrete connectors of modern life, have obscured awareness of the deeper forms by which places are connected: ridgelines, arroyos, creeks, and canyons.

California's Conflagrations

Wildfires start regularly in California. Most are immediately suppressed and able to be confined to under a hundred acres, a relatively small area in the wildlands. In some cases the fire will be monitored and allowed to burn as a controlled or "prescribed" fire. But when the conditions of weather, wind, and difficult topography combine, a wildfire can burn out of control for days or even weeks, destroying thousands of acres.

In the summer of 1992 alone, northern California suffered two stubborn blazes in rural and forest areas that the California Department of Forestry ranks with the twenty most destructive in the state's history. In Shasta County, the Fountain fire spread over sixty-four thousand acres and burned 574 structures. In Calaveras County, at the edge of the Sierra Nevada, wildfire burned through more than seventeen thousand acres of forest, taking 117 structures (including many vacation cabins) with it.

Since the late 1950s and early 1960s, the state has experienced dozens of devastating fires in the wildland-urban interface. This new phenomenon of fire bursting out of the wildlands into suburban housing developments is a product of the building boom of those decades. Extending the suburbs, developers found choice building sites on hillsides and ridges. Exclusive and rustic, the locations now sound like a wildland firefighter's nightmare: Winding streets following the topography climb to a ridgetop, whose narrow "hogback" apex has been graded flat. At the summit, streets are laid out that end in cul-de-sacs to enhance privacy. Houses are cantilevered over canyons, whose steep slopes are dense with natural vegetation. The danger signals for firefighters are lack of access; the tendency of fire to sweep up a slope, trapping victims and houses on the tops of hogback ridges; and the "fuel path" of vegetation leading straight to overhanging decks and porches.

In 1961 the skies of Los Angeles filled with black smoke and a dull, orange glow when the Bel Air fire blazed out of a brushy canyon in the Santa Monica Mountains and destroyed 484 high-priced homes. The densely populated Los Angeles basin is ringed with dry, rugged mountains, which form the figurative and, in some cases, literal backyard for the region's cities. In fact, L.A.'s most prized living areas are the canyons and hilltops.

In 1977 the Sycamore Canyon fire in Santa Barbara burned more than 200 houses in the exclusive Montecito district and threatened hundreds more before a wind shift helped firefighters bring it under control. Santa Barbara, a coastal town framed by a steep curtain of mountains behind it, often has been vulnerable to fire, especially when the wind blows out of the dry northeast instead of from the sea. Fire had swept down the steep mountain into Montecito before, in 1964, when the Coyote fire burned 94 homes and blew cinders all the way to the beach. And in 1961 whirling dry winds had pushed a hot fire out of the mountain canyons into avocado orchards and isolated homes and barns.

In June 1990 a conflagration known as the Painted Cave, or Paint, fire struck the Santa Barbara area, claiming the record as the state's most destructive fire until the East Bay hills fire supplanted it the following year. Starting at two different locations on the edge of the Los Padres National Forest, the fire roared through a dry chaparral canyon and into the suburbs. The Paint fire occurred on a day of the most extreme weather conditions: temperature at 109 degrees and humidity at 9 percent. Despite the fact that firefighting forces were on alert due to the critical conditions, the fire burned 641 structures and forty-nine hundred acres before it was stopped.

Within three days of the Painted Cave fire, three other major wildland fires raged in southern California: the Glendale College Hills fire burned 64 homes on Los Angeles's eastern edge, the Carbon Canyon fire burned through undeveloped areas of Orange and San Bernardino counties, and a major fire flared from a controlled burn in Riverside County.

The common factor connecting these conflagrations, beyond the elements of topography, vegetation, and weather, is that of surprise: disbelief that the security of one's established, built community could be so susceptible to the forces of nature. This disbelief fueled the shock that followed the East Bay hills fire of October 20, 1991, despite a history of similar fires in the same area.

The Day of the Fire

Critical Fire Weather

The day of the fire in the East Bay hills, Berkeley and Oakland experienced record-high temperatures, eighty to ninety degrees. The unusual hot, dry wind blowing from the northeast lowered the humidity to 16 percent, a dramatic drop from the 25 to 35 percent that is typical for the Bay Area. These *foehn* winds, similar to the Santa Ana winds of southern California, blow out of the state's hot interior. They occur rarely—perhaps six to ten days a year. Normally, the San Francisco Bay Area is cooled by the marine layer, borne on southwesterly winds from the Pacific Ocean. Coastal mountains act as a barricade against the scorching summer climate of the vast agricultural Central Valley to the east. In fact, that summer had been a particularly cool one for the Bay Area, with week after week of spirit-dampening overcast instead of the sun.

Although September and October are typically the months when the summer fog lifts and the days are warm, it is always a warmth tinged with autumn. So the promise of a delectable summery day on a Sunday in late October must have been more tempting than usual for sun-starved Berkeleyans. But the odd *diablo* wind, as it was called later, blowing from the direction of Mount Diablo to the east, put an apprehensive edge on enjoyment of the Indian summer weather, and people spoke of an "ominous" feeling as the wind blew stronger and hotter and the day moved toward noon. The conjunction of high temperatures, wind from the northeast, low humidity, and bone-dry vegetation, parched from five years of drought and the past winter's killing freeze, created a deadly mix known to wildland firefighters as "critical fire weather." While these factors do not ignite fires, they support their spread and inhibit quick suppression.

"The weather conditions that day were explosive, with severe winds and tinder dryness," said Berkeley Fire Chief Gary Cates. "The fuels—that is, vegetation—were as close to gasoline as you could get with solid material. The low humidity caused the combustible materials to explode when they caught fire, and then, carried on the wind, they spread. When the stand of eucalyptus east of Hiller Highlands ignited and the fire reached the crowns, the wind spread literally millions of little flaming missiles in a southwesterly direction.

"There is a window of conflagration," the fire chief continued, "that occurs when the various elements circling in the cosmos line up: temperature, humidity, and wind. When they get lined up and a fire occurs, it's 'Katie, bar the door!' "

The original fire started the afternoon before, on Saturday the nineteenth, and burned three hillside acres of dry grass in a canyon between Buckingham Boulevard and Marlborough Terrace in Oakland, just downhill from Grizzly Peak Boulevard, which runs along regional park open space. Smoke from the grass fire was visible from the University of California's Memorial Stadium in Berkeley, where a football game was going on, the sixth-ranked Cal Bears against the number-one-ranked University of Washington Huskies. Spectators in the filled-to-capacity stadium said later that they noticed the smoke and felt uneasy, but then thought no more about it.

However, City Manager Mike Brown, Fire Chief Cates, and Fire Marshal Gary Bard were worried. The city manager and the fire marshal, who were both attending the game, left in the middle of the first quarter and conferred at the mobile police van parked outside the stadium. They understood the ordinary logistical problems of moving some seventy thousand football fans in and out of the area for a regular home game, so they were concerned about the prospect of evacuation in the event of fire on Panoramic Hill just above. Bard then joined Chief Cates and Deputy Chief Dan Salter at the fire department office and for most of the football game maintained a full alert. "I didn't get back to the stadium until the fourth quarter," Bard recalled. "Cal lost but it was a close game."

The wind that day was minimal, and the fire was apparently stopped by late afternoon. No one knows the cause of the Saturday fire, but had it occurred two days later, under normal westerly-wind conditions, rather than during the "window of conflagration," the chances are good that it could have been completely contained.

Instead, Sunday the twentieth dawned hot and clear, with no usual morning coolness. By 6:00 A.M. the humidity was so low that water sprinkled on the ground evaporated immediately. When Oakland and East Bay Regional Parks firefighters returned Sunday morning to check on the burn area of the Saturday fire and to gather up their hoses, they found tendrils of smoke coming from the deep layer of burned vegetation, known as duff. The air was so hot and dry that when they attempted to wet down the hot spots, the water evaporated before it could penetrate the duff. Suddenly, just before 11:00 A.M., the wind grew stronger and carried burning embers beyond the perimeter of the already-burned area, setting fire to dry grasses. Within seconds the wind whipped the fire out of control and it flashed across a distance as large as a football field, igniting trees like torches and overwhelming the firefighters.

Then, within only thirty minutes, driven by the strong winds, the fire engulfed the canyon and blew straight out along the ridgeline, swept through Hiller Highlands, and burned down along the ridge, following the descending elevation to its lowest point and pushing the massive fire front across Tunnel Road and Chabot Road to the other side of Highway 24.

The Devil Wind

The fire was felt under the skin before it was seen. That Sunday morning in the hours before the fire swept through their neighborhood, the people on Alvarado and Vicente roads puzzled at the unusual early-morning heat and incessant wind. Their uneasiness switched to alarm as they realized that the nearby hills were on fire.

The light coming through the skylight was bright and sunny when Jeff Grote stepped into the shower shortly after eleven o'clock. Suddenly, the light changed to a deep amber and the sky outside darkened.

Grote's neighbor, Carl Goetsch, had a similar experience. "I was in the shower. The first thing I was aware of was a strange yellow light coming through the skylight in the bathroom. I stepped out and saw a huge column of smoke and flame coming from the hill behind."

One street over, Esther Hirsh was preparing to go to her law office in San Francisco. "I was late, so I was hurrying to take a shower and get ready. When I was in the shower I glanced out the bathroom window and saw that the sky was dark. I thought it was odd, because earlier it had been a bright, sunny, windy day."

"It was a very strange morning," Jeff Grote recalled. "There was a hot, twitching wind—sort of a devil wind. My wife had said, 'Do you think we need to worry about fire?'"

Esther Hirsh remembered having an ominous feeling when she was outside earlier in the day with her baby daughter, Natalie. "At eight-thirty or nine o'clock in the morning it was strangely hot and windy. I thought that perhaps it was earthquake weather. I did not think of fire. Later, when the sky turned dark, I thought that maybe it was going to rain. There were black, roiling clouds in the sky. The next thing, my husband was running up the stairs saying, 'Esther, we've got to evacuate!'"

Where There's Smoke . . .

At first the smoke billowing in white cloud plumes above the hills to the south, visible behind Radston's Office Supply across the street, was a curiosity to the A shift at Berkeley Fire Station 2. Station 2 is the closest firehouse to Berkeley's downtown and for years served as one of the headquarters for on-duty assistant fire chiefs. It functions as the emotional locus for the force, the home turf that the current drab administration building, set in a civic complex of public buildings, never could be.

It was Sunday morning, normally a peaceful time in a firehouse. The crew of Engine 2 had just returned from a fire alarm call at a student residence on Channing Way: a sprinkler head in a laundry chute set off by a malfunctioning smoke alarm. They had gone twice on the false alarm, missing the ritual Sunday breakfast, which they ate cold at eleven o'clock, the last meal they were to have that day. On the drive back to the station the second time, Captain David Orth observed to his engine company, "If we get a fire today there'll be hell to pay." Orth was familiar with the Santa Ana winds in southern California and the Gaviotas in Santa Barbara County, and he was troubled by the hot, dry winds gusting along Berkeley's streets that morning, sending swirls of trash in all directions.

The gusty winds scratched at the instinctive alert mechanisms of other Berkeley firefighters too, overriding any prospect of relishing a warm, summery day. Captain Wayne Dismuke, coming on duty at 7:00 A.M. as acting assistant fire chief for the day, worried that if there were a fire "it would mean trouble." Briefed by the officer going off-shift about Oakland's grass fire of the day before, he learned that Engines 3 and 5, the Berkeley fire companies closest to the Oakland border, had been called to provide aid to Oakland. At 9:00 A.M. Dismuke told the Engine 3 crew to stand by in case Oakland called for direct aid again.

Berkeley Fire Station 3 is located near College Avenue, on Russell Street, just three blocks down the street from the landmark Claremont Hotel. The fact that the Claremont stands in Oakland is an anomaly that has frustrated the

Berkeley Fire Department, since the hotel is closer to Station 3 than to any Oakland fire company. The Oakland city line was thrown lasso-like around the Claremont and the hills behind it years ago in a maneuver inspired by lust for tax revenues. The result is a Berkeley-Oakland boundary that cuts arbitrarily back and forth through the Claremont hills. The residents of those hills who technically live in Oakland nevertheless have a Berkeley zip code, further confusing their civic identity.

Station 3's Acting Lieutenant Brian Corrigan, a veteran of wildland firefighting (from his experience as a seasonal ranger with the California Department of Forestry), tossed lightweight, fireproof brush gear into Engine 3 in anticipation of a brush fire call. He got out maps of Berkeley's "hazardous hill area," so called because of its proximity to fire-prone wildlands, and reviewed with his crew the streets they might encounter. Corrigan noted later

Smoke billowing across the sky to the south was the first sign of the fire visible from Berkeley Fire Station 2. Photo by John Anderson.

that they studied Panoramic Hill, tangent to the University of California's Strawberry Canyon, and north of the eventual reaches of this fire. The hazardous hill zone at that time did not include the area of Berkeley that burned. Since the fire, the hazardous zone boundaries have been expanded. He also noted that the Berkeley Fire Department's map books do not include Oakland and that Berkeley crews consult regular street maps on mutual aid calls to other cities.

Corrigan then called Lieutenant Charlie Miller at Station 5 to ask if the four-wheel-drive vehicle, used in attacking grass fires, was ready to go. "We were not ostriches," declared Miller later. "Most of the Berkeley Fire Department was on alert status because of what had occurred the day before."

There is a radio scanner at Fire Station 3, the personal property of Lieutenant Mickey Gray. It is a commentary on the diminished state of public funding for the fire department that only two scanners—at Station 2 and Station 5—had been bought by the department. After receiving Dismuke's standby call, Corrigan tuned in the scanner and shortly before eleven o'clock "heard the fire going down" and the Oakland units being dispatched.

"I didn't think anything about it," reported Corrigan. "It sounded like just another fire, until I looked outside and saw the flag standing straight out in the stiff wind."

At Station 2 after breakfast, when the housekeeping and maintenance chores of a firehouse normally take place, the firefighters gathered on the sidewalk outside to watch the clouds of smoke. "We watched the smoke column," recalled Orth, "and periodically you'd see big, quickly rising columns of very dark smoke coming up." The black smoke was an ominous signal that another house had been elected for fiery destruction. Burning structures somewhere to the south were turning the white smoke of a grass fire into the blackening cloud that by noon blocked out the sun.

With the urgent sense that "we just wanted to go," the crew prepared for the fire that they had not yet been called to. "We were monitoring the radios intensively," said Orth. "We brought all the equipment up to the front office so we could have it in one place." They had first picked up the Oakland Fire

Department's activity on the radio scanner, listening as they watched the smoke. Now, in the office bristling with radio equipment—scanner, base station, and hand-held portables—they tuned one portable to Oakland, monitored the police on the scanner, and listened to Berkeley's dispatch center on the base station.

Still only observers, they set up a video camera in the window of the front office. The fixed shot on the videotape frames a banal street scene of the Radston's store on the corner and an empty parking lot across the street. The only movement is the smoke: first billowing white clouds of it; then, in greater and greater volume, a churning, inky mass blowing across the entire sky to the south, like an unstoppable plume escaping from an evil genie's lamp.

Finding the Fire

"It's in Oakland"

There was one major question on the firefighters' minds: Where is the fire? Dependent on that knowledge would be answers to the next questions: Will we be called for mutual aid? Does the fire threaten Berkeley? In the agonizing process of reconstituting the events of the fire in the weeks that followed, it became clear that an early impression that "the fire is in Oakland" blunted the awareness that Berkeley might be in the fire's path and hampered a coordinated response in the first hour.

On Saturday, October 19, the Oakland Fire Department had requested direct aid from Berkeley to suppress the three-acre brush fire near Marlborough Terrace and Buckingham Boulevard in the hilly Grizzly Peak area. (Oakland and Berkeley can call each other for "direct aid," whereas "mutual aid" is dispatched by a regional coordinator, so the city needing aid does not have to make all the calls itself.) Berkeley's Engine 3 went to the fire, and Engine 5, stationed at the south end of Shattuck Avenue, less than six blocks from the Berkeley-Oakland border, "covered in" at Oakland's Station 8 at 51st Street and Telegraph Avenue.

Now, on Sunday, no call came from Oakland. Afterward, hard questions were put to the two fire departments about the absence of communication between them. Acting Assistant Chief Dismuke told investigators from the California Office of Emergency Services that he assumed Oakland would call if they needed help, as they had on Saturday. Once the holocaust was under way, Dismuke said, "We were so busy. I figured they were as busy as we were." The concept of notifying an adjacent city about a spreading fire—or of calling preemptively to inquire about potential fire threat—was not as developed as the mechanism of requesting aid. "There is a longtime working relationship between the two cities," maintained Assistant Chief Paul Burastero, who was involved with deploying forces on the day of the fire, "but the problem with this fire is that we both had our heads in it."

In Oakland in the half hour between 11:00 and 11:30, the conflagration turned into certain catastrophe, with houses catching fire at a rate of one every four and a half seconds. Oakland's command structure collapsed in shock for a while when Fire Battalion Chief James Riley and police officer John Grubensky, attempting to evacuate citizens trapped behind the fire lines, were killed. In that first half hour the Oakland Fire Department, already working with a fire crew from the East Bay Regional Parks District, called for direct aid from the California Department of Forestry, because of its helitac unit and wildland equipment, and for mutual aid from the nearby cities of Alameda, Emeryville, and San Leandro and the fire departments at the Alameda Naval Air Station and the Lawrence Berkeley Laboratory. They did not call the Berkeley Fire Department, the Oakland command said later, because everyone assumed Berkeley was already busy fighting the fire.

In order to learn if the bulging cloud of smoke threatened Berkeley, the Berkeley Fire Department was on its own. Certain fire stations were monitoring the Oakland fire frequencies, but there was no direct radio contact. So Acting Assistant Chief Dismuke decided to drive into the hills to have a look for himself. Leaving Station 2 at 11:30 A.M., Dismuke took Dwight Way to Panoramic Hill, above the University of California campus. Looking south, he could see only smoke, not its source. He circled back down and picked up Claremont Avenue, which he took up to Grizzly Peak Boulevard, and drove south into Oakland. From his vantage point on the ridgeline, Dismuke could look down at the cradle of the Saturday fire and its rebirth on Sunday.

What he could not see, because of the rolling terrain, was the extent of the fire's spread, as it leaped up to the ridge that stretched to Hiller Highlands and fanned out to the south and north simultaneously.

"Our knowledge of the fire was always limited to what we could see," Berkeley Fire Chief Gary Cates said later. "And because of the wind we were all fighting the fire on constantly changing fronts."

Even what could be seen could not necessarily be communicated. The emergency radio frequencies in both Berkeley and Oakland quickly became overloaded, in some cases leaving firefighting units isolated from overall command. Telephone lines into the dispatch centers became jammed with 911 calls from the public, making it difficult for fire units to call in or for dispatchers to call out to the field. A special tactical phone line that links East Bay fire departments had been rendered useless several weeks before by the completion of a high-rise building in the path of the microwave signal. Since no regular testing of the "tac" line had ever occurred, no one knew about the outage until the fire. An East Bay Regional Parks helicopter could not get access to radio channels and was forced to land near a communications truck on the ground each time its reconnaissance crew wanted to report new fire activity.

On Grizzly Peak Boulevard, Dismuke encountered strike teams from another jurisdiction. At the time, he thought they were from the California Department of Forestry (CDF). Later, he concluded they were probably from the fire department of the East Bay Regional Parks District. Engulfed in an eerie isolation, these firefighters could have been on a pretechnology battleground— one imagines Civil War soldiers, strayed from their company—rather than on a modern fireground. In his written statement Dismuke reports:

> I turned right onto Grizzly Peak Blvd., and headed south for approximately one half mile before I came upon a CDF Strike Team; they were stopped along the west side of the road. There were approximately five units [e.g., fire engines] in this Strike Team. I was approached by a CDF

Captain who wanted to know if I was an Oakland Chief. I told him, "No": I was from Berkeley and trying to determine if Berkeley was involved or in danger of being involved in this fire. I observed heavy fire throughout the valley below Grizzly Peak Blvd. At this time, as I proceeded back to Berkeley, I encountered another CDF Strike Team. I was stopped by this Strike Team inquiring about the location of the first Strike Team. I informed them that I had seen the first team a quarter of a mile down the road; I continued on towards Berkeley.

Dismuke's reconnaissance showed him the back of the fire. He reported to the dispatch center at 11:54: "The bulk of the fire is still in Oakland . . . it doesn't appear to be close to Berkeley. But it is a big fire." The dispatcher gave him a report that had just come in from one of the Berkeley fire stations monitoring the Oakland channel: "Air tankers have been activated, the fire has now crossed Marlborough Terrace, and they have two houses involved." Dismuke confirmed, "I'm up here [in Oakland] now. I can see one of the houses burning right now."

Yet it wasn't until the first call came from a Berkeley address a few minutes after noon, reporting "fire coming over the hill," that a Berkeley fire company was dispatched. Dismuke later said, "It was now apparent to me that this large, fast-moving grass and brush fire that I had just observed was in fact endangering the city of Berkeley."

For the first hour, until that call, knowledge about the fire had been indirect and secondhand. Now, as the spreading smoke cloud darkened and the wind blew harder, alarmed calls from the public to the Berkeley dispatch center increased.

The very first calls on the fire had come at 11:06 and 11:09 from people at the fire's source, on Buckingham Boulevard in Oakland. The next call, a minute later, was from the ill-fated Parkwoods Apartments, located in the path of the fire's initial flash. These Oakland callers, desperate to know if they should evacuate, had called directly to Berkeley's fire operators, who told them, "You need to call Oakland, they'll advise you."

Where the Fire Spread

The fire surged out of the canyon in all directions. It burned up the hill to the east toward Grizzly Peak, and from there followed the ridge far to the southeast into wooded ravines in Montclair and along Broadway Terrace in the Oakland hills. It followed another ridgeline to the northwest, eventually burning through the Claremont hills of Berkeley and Oakland and down into Vicente Canyon.

In its initial spread the fire swept southeast toward the Caldecott Tunnel, consuming the Parkwoods Apartments that overlooked the freeway there. The Parkwoods was one of the few apartment complexes in a fire zone of predominantly single-family dwellings. A high number of elderly people and university students were among the mostly uninsured tenants who were displaced as the three-story complex burned to the ground and the twelve hundred residents fled, leaving behind their possessions. Only a stand of charred pine trees remains as silent testimony to the force of the inferno and the direction of the wind.

Pushing southeast along a broad fire front, the conflagration flashed across Highway 24, from the top of the Caldecott Tunnel down to the upper Rockridge district, fanning southward through Rockridge and lower Broadway Terrace. From there the fire straddled Highway 13, the old Warren Freeway, which changes its name to Tunnel Road after it crosses Highway 24 and heads into Berkeley.

Facing page: The fire leapt out of the canyon where it originated (see dot), then fanned out in all directions, following ridgelines and flashing across two concrete freeways. The shaded areas on the map show the time progression of the fire spread. Map at right: Location of the fire area in the San Francisco Bay Area. Maps adapted by Norma J. Hennessey from a map by David Kehrlein and Craig Casteneda, courtesy of the California Office of Emergency Services and from a regional map by Alison Sosna.

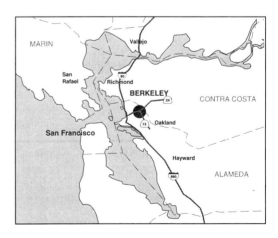

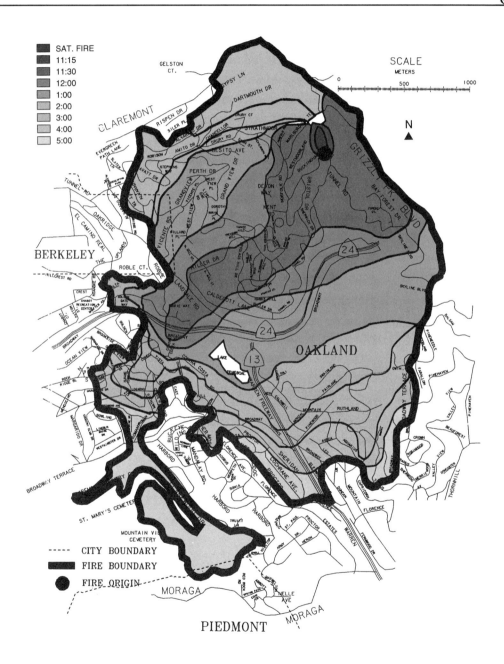

SAT. FIRE
11:15
11:30
12:00
1:00
2:00
3:00
4:00
5:00

SCALE
METERS
0   500   1000

N
▲

---- CITY BOUNDARY
▬▬ FIRE BOUNDARY
● FIRE ORIGIN

South of Tunnel Road the fire moved around to the west and then burned back north, destroying the Chabot Road area and threatening to burn through Berkeley's Roble Road neighborhood in a pincerlike movement.

Heading toward Piedmont, the fire cut across the Claremont Country Club on Broadway Terrace and the Mountain View Cemetery behind it, burning along a ridge into Piedmont's Blair Park. Piedmont firefighters held the line there, saving the town's old corporation yard on the edge of the park and preventing further spread.

On its northwest flank, the fire reached

The Parkwoods Apartments burned to the ground in the first half hour of the fire, leaving twelve hundred people homeless. Photo © 1991 Michael Mustacchi / Still News Photos.

almost to Claremont Avenue, incinerating entire sections of the Gravatt,
Alvarado, Vicente, and Grandview neighborhoods in the Berkeley-Oakland hills
above the seventy-six-year-old Claremont

Hotel—but stopped short of reaching
that venerable wood-frame structure or
continuing north into the University of
California at Berkeley.

The Berkeley dispatchers in the Public Safety Communications Center
had received two pieces of information from Acting Assistant Chief Dismuke
from his vantage point on Grizzly Peak: "The fire is in Oakland" and "If any
further developments happen or it starts to infringe on Berkeley, I'll let you
know and you can notify Chief Cates." Before starting out on his ride, Dismuke
had instructed the communications center to alert Fire Chief Cates and deputy
chiefs Billy White and Dan Salter "for notification only." So low-key was this
instruction that the dispatcher did not call the chiefs on their pocket pagers,
but telephoned their home numbers and (except for Deputy Chief Salter) left
messages on answering machines.

Now, as the barrage of calls came in from anxious residents all the way
from the flatlands of south Berkeley to the hills above the U.C. campus, the dispatchers had only the direction from Dismuke.

These calls came to the police dispatcher:

11:13   "Are you aware there's a fire in the Oakland-Berkeley hills?"

"The Oakland Fire Department is there."

11:30   "Hi, I was just looking out my window, and I see all this brown smoke,
coming out of the hills. It looks like a fire."

"Okay, whereabouts are you?"

"I'm on LeConte Street and I'm looking in the hills. It looks like it's in the Strawberry Canyon area."

"Okay, we're on the way."

11:32   "There's a fire on the . . ."

"Yes, in the hills?"

"Yeah."

11:33   "I'm calling from Panoramic Way . . ."

"Regarding the fire?"

"Yes."

"Yes, ma'am, we're responding."

11:33   "What's going on with this fire, up in the hills?"

"Oakland's there. It's Oakland, and there must just be a lot of smoke. Oakland's there . . ."

Like a mantra, the dispatchers repeated "It's in Oakland" and "Oakland's there" so many times that the words took on a reassuring quality. The repetition led to false assumptions and to embellishment: "We're responding," even though Berkeley fire engines were not sent until just after twelve o'clock. One dispatcher told caller after caller that "if they want you to evacuate, they will drive through the streets with a loudspeaker." But that is largely a police function, which the fire department usually does not handle. As streets were overwhelmed with fire, firefighters knocked on doors to be sure people were out. A frazzled dispatcher told callers, "There have been no evacuations as far as I know," twenty minutes after the first Berkeley fire officer on the scene had called in to request that evacuation be started.

Although the dispatchers were aware of the wind ("It's one of those winds again," said the fire desk dispatcher), the assumption was that the wind was exaggerating the smoke. The thought that the wind could blow the fire toward Berkeley did not come up.

By 11:30 A.M., on another dispatch desk, the calls were coming in at a rate of nearly ten calls a minute. The dispatcher responds:

11:26 "We're already aware of it. Both Oakland Fire and we're en route to it."

11:30 "Yeah, we're . . . Oakland's already en route. It's in Oakland, okay?"

11:30 "We're already en route to the fire up in the Berk . . . Oakland hills."

11:30 "Yeah, we're already en route."

11:30 "Yeah, we're already en route in the hills, ma'am."

11:30 "Yeah, ma'am, we're already en route, actually it's Oakland."

11:30 "Yeah, Oakland Fire is en route, ma'am."

11:35 "Yeah, ma'am, everybody's calling about it. There's a lot of smoke."

At 12:09 P.M. a caller asks:

". . . are we in danger? Should we be starting to water down or something?"

And the exasperated dispatcher replies:

"I really don't have an answer for you, ma'am. I don't know how far the fire is. I'm sitting in a little room answering a whole bunch of calls and I don't even have a TV set, so I don't know. I can't even call to Oakland, 'cause I have no lines out."

The whole city could see what the dispatchers, in a windowless room, could not see. Overwhelmed by the volume of 911 calls, the dispatchers dealt with the onslaught by minimizing it. It was a serious shortcoming in the operation of the communications center that no protocol existed for the dispatchers to let the officers in the field know that a great number of citizens were calling to report smoke that seemed to be very close to Berkeley, or for the fire officers to relay information that could be announced to the public. Moreover, the dispatchers were working without a supervisor. Captain Mike Corker, the fire supervisor for the communications center, normally does not work evenings and weekends. He had returned from vacation that Friday and was at home when the fire started. He called in to ask if he was needed at about 1:15 P.M., and arrived at the communications center at about 2:15. Without a supervisor and without intelligence from the field, the dispatchers had been left to rely on their own judgment in a crisis situation.

The dispatchers were overwhelmed trying to deal with the radio contacts from the fireground, the need to call other cities for direct aid, and 911 telephone calls from the public. Fire officers attempting to call in on cellular phones found the lines tied up.

The dispatch functions of Berkeley's fire and police departments had been merged into the Public Safety Communications Center in 1984. Typically there is a fire dispatcher and a police dispatcher, who handle those departments' radio traffic and dispatch operations. Two other positions answer 911 emergency calls, although the phone lines go to all four positions. Monday through Friday there is a fire department supervisor in the communications center, whose job is to make critical decisions and conduct mutual aid requests when necessary.

Before 1984 the Fire Dispatch Center, which was located at Station 2, was staffed by the firefighters themselves. Often they would have spent one or two years in the field before serving a stint as dispatchers and so were intimately familiar with firefighting practices, equipment, terminology, and the local streets. In 1976 the fire department had begun using "civilian" dispatchers, who were thoroughly incorporated into the fire operation. The quality of fire dispatch began going downhill in 1984, according to the fire department, when, forced by a shrinking budget, the city of Berkeley combined fire and police dispatch in the police headquarters. The physical move constituted a systemic change, as the budget, training, and staffing decisions were consolidated into the police department.

Wires Down: Engine 3's Costly Delay

On Engine 3, with brush gear loaded and maps studied shortly after 11:00 A.M., Acting Lieutenant Brian Corrigan was ready to go. The column of smoke was blanketing the sky directly to the south of Station 3, and Corrigan planned to take a ride up past the Claremont Hotel on Tunnel Road to investigate. A fire company is free to take exploratory drives as long as it stays in its assigned district. But by that time the wind was creating havoc knocking down tree branches, and at 11:16 a call came in to the dispatcher announcing downed electrical wires in Engine 3's zone. A live power line is a life-threatening situation, and Engine 3 had to go and stand by until utility workers from Pacific Gas & Electric Company (PG&E) could come and disconnect the line. PG&E crews were already answering calls for downed lines in other parts of the East Bay and took nearly an hour to arrive.

"We had to sit there and watch the smoke column build and build and build," said Corrigan. "It was black, so we knew houses were burning." Corrigan and his crew, driver Jarrel Jung and firefighter/paramedic Tom McGuire, were soon surrounded by a crowd of about twenty people wanting to know about the fire.

"Fire Coming Over the Hill!"

At 12:06 P.M. the first Berkeley fire call came in—"Fire is coming over the hill"—from the Grote house at 32 Vicente Road, just four houses east of Tunnel Road and downslope from the Hiller Highlands.

Engine 3 had been relieved of the wires-down vigil moments before, and, said Corrigan, "We jumped on the rig and went to the alarm." The noonday sun was completely obscured by the smoke, and Corrigan noticed the street-lights coming on as he crossed Domingo at the Claremont and started up Tunnel. His progress was slow because the road was choked with traffic.

Tunnel Road, as it heads out of Berkeley to cross Highway 24 and become Highway 13 (which runs south to the Montclair district of Oakland) is a chute-like road, divided by a concrete wall down the middle. You cannot make a left turn onto Vicente. Corrigan drove to the top of Tunnel to make a U-turn at Hiller Drive and found flames roaring across the road, surging through the dry underbrush and live oaks that line the street, and houses on both sides of the road already on fire.

Corrigan got on the radio and called for a first alarm to report to Tunnel Road and Vicente. In the Berkeley Fire Department, a first alarm calls three engine companies (each company has a pumping engine and a crew of three), one ladder truck, one paramedic ambulance, and an officer of chief's rank to the fire scene. On a second alarm, two more engines and a truck are sent. A third alarm brings in the last two on-duty engines of Berkeley's fleet. Every fire department has its own pattern of response, depending on its equipment and staffing.

Engine 3 was already part of the first-alarm response, and Corrigan told the dispatchers "to fill up the assignment and notify the chief we need mutual aid. We have multiple structures on fire. We need the police department to close Tunnel Road and start evacuating people here." He then turned back down Tunnel Road and swung the engine onto Vicente.

What Corrigan saw, looking at the row of large, two-story houses on the south side of Vicente Road, was a scene that was nearly normal. The backyards that sloped up behind the houses were planted in mature pine, redwood, and deodar cedar, making visibility to the top of the hill above extremely limited. "I saw smoke up behind 32 Vicente," Corrigan said later, "but I had no idea where it was heading. My main objective was to find out where the fire was coming from."

Corrigan's Unfortunate Mission

Corrigan announced on the radio that he would go to the back of Vicente Canyon to try to get a look at the fire. Following Vicente Road, Engine 3 passed out of Berkeley and into Oakland and continued northeast on Grandview Drive, to the junction of Perth Place and Westview Place. These roads are narrow and winding, at the bottom of a steep ravine, where houses had been individually planted to coexist with nature—some on stilts, some nestled into hillsides—as solitary refuges from urban life.

Corrigan stopped the fire engine and, standing on its step, scanned the ridge above with field glasses. "I saw fire on the ridge about a quarter of a mile from my position," he said in his report, "moving across in a southeasterly direction."

The conspicuous presence of the bright red fire engine attracted people from the surrounding Oakland houses, who, nervous about the smoke on the hill, swarmed about, waiting for instruction, warning, or some advice from the fireman. But Corrigan, observing that the fire was being blown in the opposite direction, out toward Tunnel Road, decided to join the Berkeley fire companies he knew would be arriving on Tunnel, where houses already were being threatened. When he climbed back into the truck and rolled off down the street, the people went wild. That indignation, magnified a hundredfold after their houses burned down several hours later, plagued the fire department in its relations with the public for several months after the fire. At public meetings and in letters to the fire department, Vicente Canyon residents accused Corrigan of turning back because their houses were in Oakland, not in Berkeley. Some believe they heard him say he could not stay and fight a fire in Oakland. No uninvolved person was there to record the events, but the circumstances lead to several conclusions:

1.   Corrigan followed the cardinal rule of wildfire-fighting procedures: don't commit your forces if you can't see the fire.

2.   The Oakland-Berkeley city line was not a factor in Corrigan's decision to leave. Berkeley's firefighters cross it all the time. In fact, on other fronts in this fire—Roble Road and upper Alvarado—Berkeley fire crews fought mostly in Oakland.

3.   Corrigan committed a public relations gaffe. By failing to communicate his plan to the crowd when he pulled out, he violated the confidence the fire department, as a source of authority and reassurance, has built with the public.

The Moving Fire

The Fire's Sweep: Where the Fire Traveled

The neighborhoods along the eastern edges of Berkeley and Oakland are built into the contours of the grassy hills and live-oak-and-laurel-studded canyons that reach into the East Bay Regional Parks District land and the East Bay Municipal Utility District watershed. This undeveloped open space extends north to south along a coastal ridgeline and is the line of demarcation between the metropolis of cities flung along the shore of the bay and the suburban communities in Contra Costa County to the east. The gateway to Contra Costa County is the Caldecott Tunnel, through which the Highway 24 freeway runs west to east beneath the hills to the hotter, arid climate of the other side. The October 1991 fire started on an Oakland hillside in a canyon just north of this freeway. It was not until the fire that people realized how little the overlay of human civilization—freeways, streets, city boundaries—has to do with the forces of nature. They also realized, with the advantage of their postfire perspective, how all of their separate, isolated, and unique neighborhoods were actually part of the same configuration of ridgelines and hills.

The National Fire Protection Association's *Fire Protection Handbook* (edited by Arthur E. Cote and Jim L. Linville [Quincy, Mass.: 1991]) observes that in a classic wildland-urban interface "the built-up quality of the subdivision may give a false sense of security" (p. 8.222). This irony is bitterly true in the older, well-established areas swept or threatened by the fire, such as Broadway Terrace and upper Rockridge in Oakland and the Claremont neighborhood of Berkeley. In the Claremont district entire stretches of Vicente and Alvarado roads, as well as houses on Tunnel Road, were destroyed. "We had sidewalks!" exclaimed a woman whose Vicente Road house had been built in 1926. "The way people talk about the fire area, you would think I was Little Red Riding Hood, living in the forest!"

But Vicente Road leads into a narrow canyon where houses had nestled into hillsides covered in seasonal grasses or had overlooked ravines of oak and madrone. Alvarado Road also winds out of the older neighborhood and up to the hill above Claremont Canyon, where modern houses once perched over undeveloped hillsides. Both these areas were devastated by the fire.

The hills and ridges connected the fire areas and also isolated them. In the fire's early stages, people on Vicente Road could see smoke above the ridge behind them, but not until the flames were coming over the hill did they know for certain that they were in the fire's path.

From Vicente, Grandview Drive leads to the back of Vicente Canyon, then makes a hairpin turn and climbs south out of the canyon, along the side of the ridge, until it reaches the top. There the neighborhood suddenly changes, where the remains of Hiller Highlands stretch out ahead.

Hiller Highlands, in Oakland, with its broad, treeless streets, had more of a suburban than a rustic feel. The Highlands was a modern tract of "executive homes" and attached townhouses, carved out of a thousand-foot-high ridgetop. At the top of the hill not one structure survived the fire. Afterward, the bare hills were crisscrossed with the small, connected squares that marked the foundations of the townhouses that once had lined the streets.

Hiller commands sweeping views: west across the bay to San Francisco and the Golden Gate Bridge. From here Highway 24 looks like a child's toy track of tiny cars winding through the dense urban scene below toward the San

Francisco–Oakland Bay Bridge. The main street, Hiller Drive, drops off so steeply it seems to funnel down toward Tunnel Road, hundreds of feet below. There, miraculously, some houses remain standing. The fire swept right over them, scorching the crowns of surrounding eucalyptus trees. In their midst is the Kaiser Elementary School, which also survived. Across the street a grove of Monterey pines shields the white clapboard buildings of the private Bentley School, which was rebuilt in a record five months' time after some of its major structures were reduced to cinders.

From this vantage point, looking out at the bay, it is hard to see where the fire came from and where the fire traveled. Yet in the first devastating half hour of the blaze, most of Hiller was wiped out. After an hour it was nearly all gone. The answer lies on the other side of the ridge, to the northeast.

Turning off Hiller Drive onto Charing Cross, you leave the broad streets and graded lots of the subdivision and suddenly you remember that you are in the hills. Charing Cross, following the contour of the hill in a northeasterly direction, abruptly turns narrow and winding. A canyon opens up below. It is here that the fire started, and flashed up the hillsides to the ridgetops and from there spread out in a fan of destruction.

Charing Cross twists down to Buckingham Boulevard, which runs along the north side of the canyon, and to Old Tunnel Road, which zigzags out to the south, overlooking Highway 24 at the Caldecott Tunnel. Above Buckingham, Marlborough Terrace climbs to meet Grizzly Peak Boulevard, which runs along the north-south spine of the major hill range, forming the back of the canyon. Suddenly, it is clear: this is where the people died! They clamored to escape the killer canyon, but the switchback streets, clogged with cars and too narrow to begin with, became death traps.

It is amazing to see the number of houses that were built here. The charred pads that dot the hills on both sides of the road veer up steeply and slope off at dramatic angles that suggest wedge-shaped houses. Stands of thin, blackened pines cover the hillsides. One can readily imagine the fire sweeping through these trees and up the steep slopes to burst out of the canyon.

How the Fire Spread

The intense heat raised the temperatures of adjacent areas so that preheated telephone poles, trees, and houses exploded into flame by radiant heat transfer—even before the fire front had reached them. Radiant heat transfer from fires burning on the ground ignited the crowns of trees above. When the fire was at its height, this "fireflash" phenomenon made the fire impossible to control.

Wind was such a critical factor that by 1:00 P.M., two hours after its start, the fire had fanned out on both sides of its original path, tripling the fire area. Swirling, gusting, and abruptly shifting winds carried firebrands—burning material from trees and roofs—across canyons and concrete freeways, igniting "spot fires" that spread to an ever-widening area. One air tanker pilot reported seeing a blazing shingle fly past him at an altitude of two thousand feet. The wind carried firebrands and embers far beyond the perimeter of the blaze, starting fires on roofs, in treetops, and in dry brush on the ground. This phenomenon, which fire-fighters call "spotting," was a large element in the spread of the fire. These fires then burned back to the advancing fire front, trapping houses and threatening firefighters.

The hilly terrain exacerbated the effects of erratic wind. Because wind velocity is greater on ridgetops, the fire's movement was accelerated along the three fingerlike ridgelines that stretch northwest, southwest, and southeast. The topography of narrow canyons and abruptly cresting ridges created the microconditions for eddying winds that blew in all directions. Also, fire typically moves about 20 percent faster uphill than downhill. Flames moving uphill preheat the fuels above, accelerating combustion and firespread. And the steeper the slope, the greater the length of the flame, because the incline shortens the distance between the fire and the vegetation in its path. But in this fire the flames raced downhill as fast as they burned up. Firefighters claimed that the firestorm "broke all the rules."

Living in the Fire's Path

Meanwhile, as the Berkeley Fire Department struggled to get a sighting of the fire's direction, the residents of Berkeley's Claremont district suddenly found themselves in the fire's path. This neighborhood lies on both sides of Tunnel Road, the north-south thoroughfare that leads out of Berkeley to Oakland, becoming Highway 13. Alvarado, Vicente, and Bridge roads curve up from the east side of Tunnel. Roble Road and The Uplands veer down to the west, Roble making a dogleg turn and running straight down across the Oakland line to Chabot Road.

By approximately eleven-thirty that morning, the firestorm, driven by tornadolike winds of its own creation, was surging across the upper end of Tunnel Road in its initial sweep. It had just consumed most of Hiller Highlands and was running down the ridgeline toward the low-elevation point of Chabot Road on the west and leaping across the Highway 24 freeway to push south. It was from Chabot Road that the blaze started to burn back uphill, through Chabot Canyon and into the Roble Road neighborhood that straddles Oakland and Berkeley.

Donna and Frank Hunt looked out across Chabot Canyon from their home on Roble Road and saw the fire jumping Highway 24. When they went outside to wet down the brush and decks around their house, the retired couple suddenly realized the fire was nearly on their doorstep.

Donna Hunt: I saw the fire coming down the canyon. The swirling wind carried coals into the plantings in the median strip and caught them on fire. Soon the fire had jumped the freeway. It moved downhill faster than anybody could stop it. We thought we'd go out and water things down. I turned to look at my husband and all of a sudden it seemed the flames were just ten or fifteen feet behind him. It was a noisy, windy day and it was hard for me to get his attention. By that time our only thought was simply to get out.

Polly and John Armstrong live on lower Alvarado, on the corner of Tunnel Road, in an imposing 1920s Prairie-style house with a high, tiled roof. John is a contractor, and Polly is an aide to their local city councilman. Their daughters, Amanda and Amy, were away at college when the fire struck.

Polly Armstrong: It was Sunday morning. I was lying in bed, watching TV. The wind was blowing just tremendously. It was just around eleven when John came running upstairs and said, "There's a fire on the hillside." About twenty minutes later he came back up and said, "The wind is blowing and there's a huge fire up there. We need to think about getting out. I wish you'd get dressed so if we have to leave, we'll be ready." I turned on the radio and heard, "There is a four-alarm fire in the Oakland hills, above the Caldecott Tunnel." I looked outside, and the sky was just black.

Jeff Grote had just installed the slate roof on his Vicente Road house. The original structure, built in 1905 as the gardener's cottage for the estate on the corner of Vicente and Tunnel, had been enlarged in 1927 in the Doll's House style that was popular then. Grote, an urban planning and landscape engineer, had spent his weekends on remodeling projects ever since he and his wife, Jessie, bought the house in 1975. Daughter Alexandria, seventeen, was an infant when they moved in, and Joscelyn, thirteen, was born there. The final concrete on the last of the additions had been poured the week before the fire burned the house to the ground.

Jeff Grote: I had been at the Cal game the day before, but I didn't know about that day's grass fire. It had been a warm evening. It was a very strange morning on Sunday, with that hot sort of "devil wind" blowing. I got up and was going to go for a swim at the Claremont. Instead, I waited for my wife to come back from church. When she got home, she said, "It's a freaky morning." She wondered if we had to worry about fire. The ironic thing is we had cleared the brush on the hill behind the house and had replaced the wood-shingled roof.

The neighbors on the corner were having a christening for their baby. About eleven o'clock my kids went over to babysit for their older daughter. We decided we didn't have time for a swim before the party, and I got into the shower. Before I knew it, Jessie was calling, "There's smoke in the back!"

I looked up the hill. Now you can look all the way up the bare hill and see charred trees and foundations. Then, the hill was thick with trees and your view of the top was obscured.

Carl and Anne Goetsch lived on Vicente next door to the Grotes', in a Mediterranean-style house built in 1923. Carl and Anne are retired, with grown children. Anne remembered the 1970 fire in the Oakland hills above their home, when she worked at the University of California. She remembered how Tunnel Road was blocked off at the top and Carl couldn't get home. She had that in mind this time as she planned her strategy to get back home from church.

Anne Goetsch: When I left church I stopped to water the garden there. The wind was really strong. It almost knocked me over. It was crazy, it blew one way and then turned around and blew the other. My heart sank because I knew the disaster it could be.

Driving home, I turned off onto Alvarado rather than going up Tunnel to make the U-turn to Vicente. I remembered that in '70 Carl couldn't get home.

Our son, Alan, who is a doctor at Alta Bates Hospital in Berkeley, called and said, "Hiller Highlands is on fire. I'll come up and help you."

Fight or Flight?

The pressure to react to the threat of fire coming over the hill was intensified by uncertainty about the danger. Even when flames were in sight, disbelief that one's home could be wiped out was strong. The fire came before any public officials arrived, so there was no immediate evacuation order. For a society accustomed to experience filtered through the TV screen or the pronouncements of "specialists," this confrontation with stark reality was disconcerting and confusing. Finally, elemental self-preservation won out.

Polly Armstrong: I started walking up Tunnel Road. By then they had stopped traffic at the top, but cars were still coming up. There were lots of people outside—lots of pooling of ignorance. You couldn't see flames, but I've never seen so much smoke in my life. Tunnel Road was like a funnel, with its high sides, and smoke billowing down it.

John was inside packing. He stopped and said, "Think about what you and the children might want if we have to abandon the house." So I got all the movies and photograph albums. I had a partially packed suitcase from a recent trip. I grabbed the center part of my closet with the things I wear the most and stuffed clothes into that suitcase.

It seemed unreal. This is such a solid neighborhood. Then the cat disappeared.

The phone was ringing constantly—neighbors were saying, "What are we going to do?" No one had told us anything. John told everyone in the neighborhood they should pack.

The street was full of pedestrians. There were still no cops or firemen. I was standing on the corner of Alvarado and Tunnel. All of a sudden the top of the telephone pole across the street caught fire. There was a crown of flames. It was like the burning bush for me. I thought, if that telephone pole can burst into flames, so can my house. As I turned around, I noticed huge flames filling the sky, just above us on Tunnel, toward Bridge Road.

It was about one, twelve-thirty or one, and we took off.

Jeff Grote: I gave my younger daughter, Joscelyn, a hose to wet down the elderly neighbors' [the Goetsches'] house. We had started getting a blizzard of embers from the direction of Hiller Highlands over the hill in the back. I called next door and told Carl [Goetsch], "There's a bad fire, you've got to get out." Joscelyn was getting pretty upset. I gave her my camera and put it around her neck. I told Alexandria, my older daughter, to take what's important out of the house. She got plastic garbage bags and grabbed pictures, clothes, and scrapbooks. I said to the girls, "Go next door and get the Goetsches out." Those girls are my heroes.

Carl Goetsch: The first thing I did was gather up all the family silver. By then our son had arrived with his pickup and Anne had gotten home. Alan gathered up the Audubon prints. I was aware that even though they were not intrinsically valuable, they would be lost forever.

The Grote girls came in. They ran through the house and took off most of the family pictures hanging on the walls. I began to go through the house, gathering things up. The things I didn't take were things that I knew were insured. I could have made better choices with a dry run.

Anne Goetsch: I felt totally convinced we'd come back and find something. I never believed we'd come back to hot ashes. We salvaged almost nothing.

Jeff Grote: By that time there was chaos out on the street, reporters were milling around. I said to my wife, "You'd better call 911." That was at 12:07.

The Grotes' call was the first fire call received in Berkeley and prompted Engine 3 to respond to Vicente.

Jeff Grote: I was in the back and heard horns beeping frantically from Hiller. All of a sudden they stopped. I got a chill from the thought of what must be going on up there. I told Jessie, "Get the kids and get out." Finally, at about twelve-thirty, the family left. Jessie and Alex both drove a car out. I stayed to fight the fire.

Fighting the Fire

Orth Establishes Tunnel Command

Berkeley Fire Engines 2 and 5, Fire Truck 5, and Paramedic Ambulance 113 answered Lieutenant Brian Corrigan's first-alarm call at 12:13 P.M., reporting they were en route to Tunnel Road and Vicente. The fire rigs converged on the scene amidst a flurry of radio traffic and disarray in the streets. Acting Assistant Chief Dismuke, as the chief officer in the first-alarm response, radioed that he was heading down Claremont Canyon from his reconnaissance mission on Grizzly Peak to join the command.

Nearing the Claremont Hotel, where Ashby Avenue becomes Tunnel Road, Captain David Orth's Engine 2 made its way through the heavy traffic. Local residents who had been caught away from home when the fire started were trying to go back up Tunnel to reach their houses. Cars that had just passed through the path of the firestorm at the Caldecott Tunnel and turned off Highway 24 at Tunnel Road streamed down the road, their drivers and passengers wild-eyed and full of warnings—"Don't go up there!" At one point Engine 2, driving in tandem with Fire Truck 5, was completely stopped when a small car wedged itself beneath the rear axle, as if to hitch a ride up the hill.

Firefighter/Paramedic Robert Young, on Ambulance 113 with Luis Ponce, called in from Alta Bates Hospital, ten blocks down Ashby, that the hospital was already receiving "walk-in wounded" from the fire. He got permission from Corrigan, still the commanding officer on the scene, to call a countywide yellow alert for ambulance and hospital readiness. Paramedic 113's role on Tunnel Road would be to set up a casualty collection and triage post. Arriving at Tunnel, Young reported that he saw about fifty people standing in the street watching the fire and wondered if the medics should begin evacuation. At that moment he announced on his radio, "BPD [Berkeley Police Department] just passed by." Then, before they could set up their medical post at Tunnel and Bridge roads, the ambulance crew became involved helping police block off streets for emergency ambulance routes and assisting with evacuations.

At 12:25 P.M. Corrigan radioed that since he was heading toward Grandview to scout out the fire and would not be on the scene at Tunnel Road, he was passing command of the incident to Captain Orth. "Passing command" is an official term in the fire department's protocols. It is part of the "incident command system," which assigns responsibility for a situation to the first officer who arrives on the scene and, as in this case, defines exactly when that command is passed to another. The structure is at once flexible and specific.

"I took command and declared it Tunnel Command," said Orth in his written statement. To arrive at the "command post" at Tunnel and Vicente, Orth made the loop at the top of Tunnel Road, finding fire above and below him.

"Fire was threatening the houses at the end of Tunnel between Vicente and Hiller," he said afterward. "From the high side of Tunnel, I could see fire through the trees in the area of Roble Road. The fire was crossing the road like a horizontal blowtorch."

Engine 5, under the command of Lieutenant Charlie Miller, a twenty-year veteran of the department, arrived just ahead of Engine 2. Miller also noticed the fire raging through the wooded lots on the low side of Tunnel Road, threatening houses there and on Roble Road. Sent down to check out the area and to fight the fire along that front, Miller established Roble Command. Truck 5, operated by Wayne Lynch and John Higgings, joined Engine 5 in

Fire apparatus stretched down Ashby Avenue at the Ashby-Claremont staging area. Photo by Jane Scherr.

Roble Command and set up operations at the intersection of Tunnel and The Uplands. Truck 5's officer, Hurey Clark, was sent to the high side of Tunnel to try to save one of the houses that was burning between Hiller Drive and Vicente. There he joined the crew of Engine 4 when they arrived with the second alarm. It was soon apparent that the fire had swept around and was threatening the entire area below Tunnel Road: Roble Road and Roble Court on one spur and The Uplands, El Camino Real, Hillcrest Road, and Roanoke Road on another.

Arriving at Tunnel and Vicente, Orth immediately ordered a second alarm (which consisted of Engines 1 and 4 and Fire Truck 2) to report to Ashby and Domingo and to use the side streets of Domingo and Claremont Avenue in front of the Claremont Hotel as a staging area.

By this time, about 12:30, Dismuke had joined Orth at the command post at Tunnel and Vicente. To maintain their functions within the command structure, Dismuke declared himself Incident Commander and Orth Operations Officer. Sitting together in the cab of Engine 2, talking at once on the rig radio and a portable radio, Orth planned the strategy and deployed the forces, while Dismuke made the calls for reinforcements. Within a few minutes they called for a third alarm.

The third alarm pulled the remaining on-duty Berkeley fire companies, Engines 6 and 7, and Paramedic Ambulances 112 and 114 to the fire. The companies were already on alert, having moved to the downtown stations, Station 2 and Station 5, after the first alarm. The next step, to ensure that the rest of the city had fire protection, was to send the two reserve engines "to cover in" at the downtown stations once they were staffed by returning off-duty firefighters.

The fire spread through much of the area bisected by Tunnel Road. Map reproduced with permission granted by THOMAS BROS. MAPS. *It is unlawful to copy or reproduce all or any part thereof, whether for personal use or resale, without permission.*

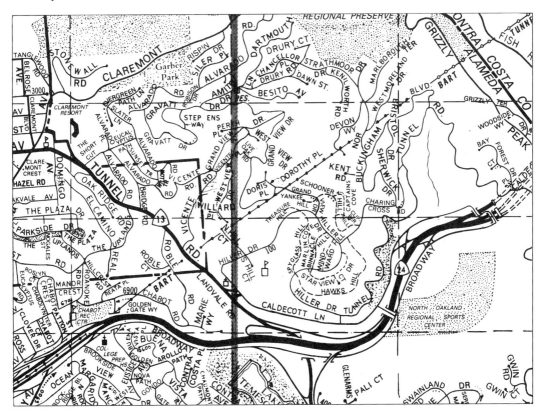

The dispatch center announced that Fire Chief Cates had just telephoned in and ordered a "recall" of off-duty officers and firefighters. Deputy Chief Dan Salter also called in from his car radio as he drove into Berkeley from his home east of the Caldecott Tunnel in Contra Costa County. He could see the large fire blazing on both sides of Highway 24. "It's much larger than you probably realize," Salter told Tunnel Command. "It's on a very broad front. Be very much aware of the thing running over you and be prepared to withdraw."

Frenzied winds spread the fire with lightning speed and turned it into a stormlike phenomenon. Eyewitnesses compared it to a tornado. The most eerie thing, they said, was the roar. Sucking in surrounding air to replace burned-up oxygen, the fire created its own wind. The more fiercely the fire burned, the more air it drew, feeding the combustion process for an even bigger, faster, and hotter fire. This phenomenon—a fire-generated wind that supersedes the force and direction of the existing wind—is called a "firestorm." The fuel load of densely built structures and dry vegetation burned so intensely that the fire reached an estimated two thousand degrees. Superheated thermal columns pulled up flaming debris and were bent ninety degrees by gale force winds into a moving horizontal wall of raging fire.

With the fire blasting around them, Orth and Dismuke realized that, for the moment at least, they were isolated from the efforts being waged on the greater fire front sweeping through Oakland. It would do no good to call on Oakland in its role as mutual aid coordinator for northern Alameda County. Shortly before 1:00 P.M., Dismuke got on the radio to the communications center and instructed the dispatcher to call the neighboring fire departments at the Lawrence Berkeley Laboratory and the city of Albany for direct aid. Minutes later, he and Orth told the communications center to order two strike teams. (A strike team is a group of five engines or five trucks of the same specifications. Strike teams are assembled for major incidents and usually are composed of vehicles from different fire departments.) He also asked for whatever other engine companies the dispatcher could find from Emeryville, Piedmont, or Alameda. By that time Fire Chief Cates had arrived at the communications center. The fire chief placed the call himself for the two strike teams, phoning

directly to the Alameda County mutual aid coordinator, the Lawrence Livermore Laboratory, located in the farmland of eastern Alameda County. The chief was told it would be at least an hour before the strike teams arrived. Half an hour after Cates's call to Livermore, Dismuke and Orth relayed a request from Corrigan, who was battling the fire on Vicente, for two more strike teams, adding that the dispatcher should try to double the order. The dispatcher estimated that it could take two hours for those strike teams to arrive. "Do the best you can. I appreciate it. Just do the best you can," said Dismuke.

Chief Cates met City Manager Michael Brown at the communications center, and together they established the city's Emergency Operations Center (EOC) in accordance with Berkeley's standby emergency operations plan. City Manager Brown was on the telephone notifying the mayor, city council mem-

City Manager Mike Brown briefs staff at the Emergency Operations Center. Fire Chief Gary L. Cates is seated on the right. Photo by Jane Scherr.

bers, and key city staff people of the disaster and the need to report to the EOC. Brown's secretary, Sandy Englund, arrived in the afternoon to help with the calling. Englund, whose father, Chet Moller, had been Berkeley's fire chief thirty years before, had a fine sense of what to do in this kind of emergency. Shortly after 1:00 P.M. Deputy Fire Chief Salter and Assistant City Manager for Public Works Jordan Rich arrived. With their arrival the core of a fire department–city hall emergency operations team was in place.

At about 1:30 City Councilman Alan Goldfarb, the acting mayor, reached the EOC. (The mayor was at an out-of-town conference that weekend.) Goldfarb's involvement in the emergency operations was especially appropriate because of his role on the city council as an advocate for earthquake and emergency preparedness. His district borders the hills on the north side of the university campus and has the sizable Hayward Fault running beneath it.

Juggling the incessant radio communications from the Berkeley firefighters on the front with outgoing telephone calls to neighboring fire departments, the overwhelmed dispatcher in the communications center managed to track down some reinforcements. But the requests from the field came incrementally, as the magnitude of the fire became evident. When they came, the dispatcher found that resources had already been committed to the fire in Oakland. Berkeley's requests for direct aid sometimes were overridden by the mutual aid system. (An engine promised by Albany was redirected to Oakland by the county mutual aid coordinator.) Strike teams never materialized until much later in the effort. Orth admits to pirating a strike team passing through Berkeley on its way to the Oakland front.

At almost 1:30 Chief Cates assigned the mutual aid function to Assistant Chief Paul Burastero, who assumed the role of logistics officer. They agreed that Berkeley High School, located near downtown, would be used as the staging area for mutual aid fire apparatus arriving in Berkeley. The site later was used as a base camp and rest area for firefighters.

At 1:53 P.M., Burastero advised Tunnel Command that he was sending Engine 7, which had been called to an apartment house fire in south Berkeley, back to the fire area to be a roving patrol for spot fires.

Dismuke: Okay, we're up here on Tunnel and Vicente. This thing is starting to crawl up above us. We've got lots of fire up here. We need all the manpower we can get, as soon as we can get it.

Burastero: Affirm. I need to hold some companies back to cover the rest of the city. If I send you both reserve rigs, we're gonna be tapped out totally.

Dismuke: Well, if we don't get somebody up here, we ain't gonna have any city to save.

Overrun on Vicente

When Engine 3 attempted to drive back out on Vicente Road to join Tunnel Command, Corrigan found the fire had gotten there first. Houses on the south side of the street, at the base of the ridge, were on fire, and the wind was whipping up the blaze.

"We saw spot fires everywhere," he said. Flying firebrands were landing on rooftops and in yards, igniting new fires every few seconds. Corrigan found a hydrant and hooked Engine 3's supply hose and began to fight house-to-house. "We were going up and down the street putting out roof fires," Corrigan recalled, "while the fire was raining down on us. One house would be under control and suddenly the house next door was on fire." The crews worked their way down the street, banging on doors as they went to be sure no people were left in the doomed houses.

Engine 3 was joined on Vicente by Engine 1 and Albany Engine 25. "I called for ten engines—two strike teams—for this street alone," said Corrigan, "but they never arrived while we were still on Vicente." The engines spread out about fifty feet apart, with the Albany engine hooked to a hydrant on Tunnel Road. The firefighters dragged lines up driveways, trying to protect the houses that had not yet ignited.

"The fire was spreading very rapidly," said Firefighter Richard Ellison, who, with Mark Mestrovich, was part of the crew of Engine 1. "I directed civilians who were there to man one of the hot lines." A number of hand-held, one-and-a-half-inch hose lines were in use on Vicente, with citizens working side by side with firefighters. The radiant heat grew so intense that even without direct fire spread or a flying brand to carry it, the fire suddenly flashed across the street, and the preheated houses there burst into flames, windows exploding.

"The fire moved right on over our heads," said Corrigan. "At one point we were surrounded on 360 degrees by fire."

After furiously working for nearly an hour, the firefighters knew they could not save the street. At 1:33 the Albany crew radioed to Tunnel Command: "We're up here on Vicente with Engine 1 and it looks like it's gonna roll over us at any time."

Captain David Orth walked up the street from Tunnel Road and had a face-to-face briefing from Corrigan. "I ordered Brian to disconnect and I

Engine 3's headlights beam through the smoke on Vicente Road as if it were night, although the time is about twelve-thirty in the afternoon. Photo by Kendra Luck.

pulled the crews off," said Orth. "All the houses were on fire and it was blowing across. I felt it was indefensible and he would die."

A Unified Command

When Chief Cates left the Emergency Operations Center at 2:00 P.M. as the fire was still raging, he took City Manager Mike Brown and Councilman Alan Goldfarb with him to reconnoiter the fire area. They drove down to the Roble Road–El Camino fire front and up across Tunnel Road past Alvarado and Bridge, talking to the firefighters along the line. They drove out Tunnel toward Highway 24 and circled east to the destroyed Parkwoods Apartments. On the way back they stopped and met with the strike team leader from San Francisco who was defending the Claremont Hotel.

After dropping off the city officials, Cates went back out in his car to the Oakland Command post that had been set up on Highway 24 in a mobile communications trailer. He met with his Oakland counterpart, Chief Lamont Ewell, and Oakland Assistant Fire Chief John Baker. He also found that Assistant Fire Chief Thomas Tarp of the California Department of Forestry was there. Together with the fire chief of Piedmont, Ron Christensen, the chiefs decided to form a Unified Command in order to create an overall strategy to stop the fire spread and allocate firefighting resources.

"We needed to know where the fire was, who was fighting it, what forces we had, and how we would deploy them," said Berkeley Fire Marshal Gary Bard, who later became Berkeley's representative in the Unified Command. "We applied the incident command system that Berkeley's firefighters use to assign responsibility at the fire scene to the entire fire area of Oakland, Berkeley, and Piedmont, dividing it into branches and divisions."

The value of a unified incident command is that it provides common procedures and common terminology for firefighters coming from different places to one fire scene. If someone asks for a "tanker," everyone understands that the request is for an air tanker, not a piece of equipment on the ground.

Berkeley Fire Marshal Gary Bard (third from left) meets with other fire officials at the Oakland Command post, set up in the middle of the Highway 24 freeway. Photo © 1991 Michael Mustacchi / Still News Photos.

When a "strike team" is ordered—five engines with a certain level of staffing and pumping capacity—a lesser grouping could leave a hole in a vital fire line.

The coordination of many different fire departments went as smoothly as circumstances allowed. Working under siege conditions, individual fire companies were sometimes unaware of which city was in command of the area where they were fighting.

"Sometimes it takes face-to-face communication at the fire scene to make a point," said Bard. "You literally have to grab someone by the shirt and speak to the person. The problem is that it takes time, and in the early stages of the fire the situation was very unstable and changed every minute."

In the beginning the Unified Command post, set up in the center of the closed-down freeway, was "just craziness," said Bard, who spent thirty-six hours there. "We were getting so much information, it was hard to separate what was really happening from what people thought was happening. It was difficult to get a handle on the fire because it was moving very, very rapidly. Fire companies would report to the command post and then start fighting the fire. Sometimes they were too busy to get back on the radio with more information for us."

The command post functioned to direct the overall operations, not to manage the strategy on the fire lines, said Bard. From the vantage point of the post, with better and better intelligence on the fire eventually coming in, the staff was able to set goals for the field commanders. Also, as hundreds of fire companies began rolling in to the area from every part of California in response to mutual aid calls, the logistics became increasingly complex.

Evacuation

A Panicky Scene

As it dawned on people that their homes were in the fire's path, they experienced a kind of "hyperreality." Whether trying to fight the fire, preparing to evacuate, or just standing transfixed, their state of shock was manifested in obsessive and sometimes bizarre behavior.

The oncoming conflagration forced everyone into action. No matter how deliberate the actions taken, in the fire's aftermath many evacuees were flooded with thoughts about what they wished they had done differently.

Esther Hirsh and Greg Nachtwey lived with their one-year-old daughter, Natalie, on Alvarado Road in a stately house built in 1924. Esther is an attorney and Greg is an investment counselor.

Esther Hirsh: There was a panicky scene on Alvarado. We took a few things and put them in the cars. We were in a state of extreme denial. Greg and I didn't think we'd lose the house. We took a few items of clothing. I thought we might be gone for a couple of days, so I grabbed a couple of things for me, for Greg, and for Natalie. We grabbed a few pictures, but not the ones that were really important. We weren't acting with foresight. We should have taken more. The pictures we lost were irreplaceable. We lost our history—baby pictures of Greg and me that our parents had given us. I did think of taking a painting that had belonged to a friend who died of AIDS last year; it had sentimental value. Greg put the painting in his car and I put Natalie in my car. Greg hosed down the roof and we secured the windows and doors.

Out on the street there were dogs running around and little boys on bikes were calling, "Get out!"

I never saw one official person, no official presence from the City of Berkeley.

It was about noon. Alvarado Road was fairly crowded with cars. Houses were burning on the ridge. A woman said, "The fire is fifteen minutes away." Everyone was saying, "Good luck."

My main thought was to get our little girl, Natalie, away from there. I didn't want her breathing the smoke. I remember the sun: it was a bright red sun. It was a horrifying sight.

Greg Nachtwey: There were fifty-mile-per-hour winds. It was very eerie. The sky was pitch black. The sun was blood red. The trees were visibly buffeted from the wind. The tremendous heat was sucking in the warm wind.

My brother, Fred, who lives on Alvarado just below us around the first turn, said the fire was going the other way. He said that fires go up canyons, not down. After we had evacuated I saw him on TV, standing on our street, wearing a surgical mask (he's a doctor), and watching the fire burn. I could identify our neighbors' fence. All I saw were flames. Then the camera panned over, and there was a straight shot of our house—in raging flames. They said it was a two-thousand-degree fire.

Esther: I didn't want to look.

Toni Garrett and Gene Farb live in a large stucco and tile-roofed house on Alvarado where the street makes a sharp turn into the burned area. They live with their two sons, Noah, age six, and baby Brian, who was one month old at the time of the fire. They are young entrepreneurs, of the sort Berkeley is famous for, who started an innovative warehouse-style household goods store that has become a local institution with several branches.

Toni Garrett: We were at swimming class at the Claremont Hotel pool that morning. I heard fire engines going up Claremont Canyon, and the instructor said, "That doesn't sound good." One of the women in the class left right then. When the class ended at eleven-thirty we saw billows of smoke and the sky got dark. I went into the shower, and when I came out at about noon we heard the Claremont had evacuated the hotel. Our whole family was there. It was scary, but none of us thought it had anything to do with us. We were in the middle of the city; you didn't anticipate that a wildfire could come down this far.

When we got home we realized it was bad. The gardeners, who were installing an irrigation system, were running the hoses to wet things down.

My little boy, Noah, was pretty scared, but he was taking care of his baby brother, Brian. I was in some state of mind. I tried to pull things out, like photographs, and we had all these people there. Everybody was yelling at me, "Get the baby out of the smoke!" I was being selective, pulling videotapes of the kids out. But you couldn't see, it was dark and the electricity was out. I had to take the tapes to the window to read the labels by the light from the fire.

When we finally left, we had about twenty minutes or so. Gene stayed for around another hour, hosing stuff down. He came out on his bicycle. The gardeners left before Gene did. It was getting scary. I saw flames at the top of the canyon above Alvarado and Vicente, probably around twelve-thirty or twelve-forty. Gene stayed until one-thirty or two. He said embers were flying around him. He rode one block on the bike, then he remembered Mr. Bird, our cockatiel, but the police wouldn't let him back in.

Anne and Stephen Walrod and their sons, Nicholas, age seventeen, and Nate, fourteen, lived on Alvarado in a large Period Revival house built in 1924, between the Farbs' and the Nachtweys'. They lost a valuable collection of rugs and artwork.

Anne Walrod: We were also at the Berkeley Tennis Club, near the Claremont. My husband, Stephen, was playing in a tournament. We heard fire engines, but we never saw them. My biggest regret is that we didn't know how serious it was. We came back home at about eleven-forty-five and we left about one o'clock. I wish we had stayed. We might have been able to save the house. I don't think it burned until much later.

Stephen was running around, activating the sprinkler system on top of the house and hosing things down. Nicholas videotaped the house. The kids were going through the house thoroughly, loading up photo albums, taking pictures off the walls. I went through the house for half an hour; I couldn't think of what to take. I put some photo albums and some rugs in the car. I was in such a state of denial I thought, "My husband is taking so much, it'll take days for me to put everything away when we get back." I thought we would be back in a couple of hours or, at least, days, so I would take a change of clothes. Stephen took suits. I was so sure the house would still be there, I just took jeans and a T-shirt. This is a city, I thought. I also thought if it were that serious, someone would have come and told us. I really lost a lot of confidence in the police and fire departments.

Stephen did see the fire on the hill across the street behind the Kusmier-skis' and the McClungs', coming very slowly. I was mesmerized. I really wanted to watch the fire. I just wanted to put a chair on the sidewalk and watch instead of packing my car. It was such a force.

When we evacuated we went to friends on Woolsey Street. We climbed up on their roof and watched the hills. Later we watched TV and saw our house burn.

Thad and Carol Kusmierski and their daughter, Anya, age twenty-two, and sons, Stefan, age twenty, and Damien, age sixteen, lived in a unique Mediterranean-style house built by Bernard Maybeck in 1928. Their lot, on Alvarado, is shaped like a piece of pie, fronting the curve of street where Vicente runs into Alvarado. Only Thad and Damien were at home the morning of the fire.

Thad Kusmierski: I was visiting down on Benvenue Street that morning. Suddenly about eleven-thirty everything went dark. People were coming down Tunnel Road from Highway 24 and the Caldecott Tunnel screaming hysterically from their cars, "Don't go up, you'll die!"

I turned on Alvarado toward the house. Everything seemed normal. I went home and put on hiking boots and climbed up to the top of the hill behind the house. I saw a panorama of fire. As I walked along the ridge I could see about a mile of fire; it seemed to be exploding.

I walked down to get the video camera. I couldn't find it, but I turned on the sprinklers and went back up the hill. Then I heard a horrendous noise, like a tornado. I turned around without a word and started running. I was glad I had boots on and I thought, "I hope I don't break a leg."

The house was dark and I woke up Damien, who was still sleeping. I walked down to Vicente. People were milling around. No one was talking. They were standing around in some sort of shock, everyone looking at everyone else, for some clue.

At that time, smoke was coming down Vicente, from the direction of Vicente Canyon. I put our dog in the car to get ready to go. I saw Anne [Walrod] closing her garage, in the process of leaving. I ran into our neighbor Bennett Markel and he said, "What a shame."

The neighborhood was known for houses of architectural and historical distinction. This was not an instant suburb, but one that was developed with a philosophy. The houses were built solidly and with great style, intended to stand the passage of years and the turns of fashion. As much as these houses were a statement of the architects' vision of permanence and esthetics, they were an expression of their owners' attainments. They were a declaration of a way of life, at once communal, or "neighborly," and highly individual. There was a continuity to the mix of periods and styles thanks to the graceful curves of the streets and the overhanging canopy of sycamore trees: turn-of-the-century Craftsman stood next to twenties Spanish Colonial next to modern houses from the forties through the present day. Several architects lost their own custom homes.

Morton McDonald's house, on the Vicente side of the Kusmierskis', was a 1910 California bungalow, said to be the first house built in the neighborhood. Next door, architect Bennett Christopherson lived with his wife, Arlyn, in a house Bennett had designed. The next house down was a 1926 Ernest Coxhead Spanish Colonial Revival with a recent library addition that Bennett Christopherson had designed for the owners, Bennett and Wendy Markel.

Bill and Karen McClung and their children, Nicola, sixteen, and John, fourteen, lived next door to the Kusmierskis' on the Alvarado side in a compact 1953 International-style house.

The lots on that stretch of Vicente and Alvarado back up to a steep, grassy hill, dotted with trees and a Victorian-style park bench. Wildflowers, blackberries, and poison oak thrive in their seasons. When McClung and his neighbors pooled resources to buy the land several years ago, McClung, a book editor, found solace and satisfaction in single-handedly carving out a trail around the south flank of the hill. Looking south, one can see into Vicente Canyon, where narrow streets converge between two steep slopes. The fire came over the hill on the far side of the canyon and then blazed its way to Vicente and Alvarado.

Bill McClung: It was extremely dry that morning. Ten minutes on the hillside would leave you parched. If you had to run downhill, you'd be parched and exhausted. I first experienced the smoke just after eleven o'clock. By eleven-thirty you could see fire coming over the top of the hill above Vicente Canyon. I left at about twelve-fifteen. The story of that last hour was one of frustration. It's too stupid. During that ill-spent hour I ran up and down the hill. I took

Berkeley's Architectural Heritage

Berkeley's founders, who created the university before they established the town, contemplated a place where the love of learning would thrive in a setting of natural beauty. The intellectuals and artists who were drawn to the university also were attracted to the lushly planted hills where fern-banked creeks run through groves of redwood, laurel, and oak. The campanile of the University of California stands against the background of these hills, identifying the city and symbolizing these twin aspects of Berkeley's character.

Berkeley's intellectual community and appealing natural setting proved a magnet for the pioneering architects of the late nineteenth and early twentieth centuries. Crowned by the university, Berkeley was known as the Athens of the West. Nationally renowned landscape designer and philosopher Frederick Law Olmsted conceived of the contoured street design of the hill communities; John Galen Howard left his stamp on the layout and the Beaux Arts edifices of the University of California campus, as well as on the town's commercial buildings; Julia Morgan built numerous public buildings and private residences; and Bernard Maybeck

pioneered and personalized residential architecture for Berkeley over several decades.

The turn-of-the-century Craftsman esthetic—houses constructed of natural materials and situated in harmony with their surroundings—found generous expression in Berkeley in the architecture of Morgan and Maybeck. In fact, the image of the brown-shingled house, set amidst an informal tangle of flowers and overhung by trees, is as much an icon for Berkeley as the campanile.

By the early 1900s, subdivision of the hills both north and south of the University of California campus was under way. In 1905 the Mason-McDuffie realty company subdivided Claremont Park, the wooded area in the Berkeley hills above the Claremont Hotel, on the south side of the campus. Real estate pioneer Duncan McDuffie hired Olmsted to create a plan of winding streets and gracious landscaping that was in keeping with the natural setting. The result was a neighborhood prized for the parklike quality of its curved roads and established street trees.

The notable early architects, Morgan, Maybeck, and Howard, as well as John

This 1909 George Plowman Craftsman, one of the oldest houses in the Claremont district, was the home of Debbie and Michael Lesser and their children. Photo courtesy of the Lesser family.

Hudson Thomas, Henry Gutterson, and Ernest Coxhead, built distinctive houses in the Claremont district. Later, in the thirties, forties, and fifties, William Wurster and Robert Ratcliff were among the modern architects whose houses were added. Together, they left a legacy of architectural classics in an eclectic mix of styles. Craftsman, Tudor Revival, Spanish Colonial, and Prairie designs coexisted in a common setting, as did the later renditions of International and other modern styles.

hoses up the hill to try to wet things down. They got all gnarled up; it was a totally fruitless effort. In the house my daughter, Nicola, filled up all the basins with water. When I came running down I slipped and fell and sprained my shoulder. So, when we finally evacuated I was too exhausted to make rational decisions. I took worthless things, like old clothes. I decided, "I can't carry my whole life down the hill."

Nicola McClung: I took my picture albums. I never thought our house would burn. It was embarrassing. You usually don't walk down the street carrying your albums.

I grabbed one cat and I went to the Claremont. People were laughing there. Later I realized it was possible that our house had burned down.

For Carol Kusmierski and Karen McClung, the anxiety they felt the morning of the fire was heightened because the two women were away from home and their families when the fire started. Carol and her daughter, Anya, were in Santa Cruz, some hundred miles away. They saw a report on the news Saturday night, but did not think it involved Berkeley. "When I got a call from a friend the next day that the fire was out of control, I drove back faster than I ever had before," said Carol. The drive from Santa Cruz to the East Bay involves a treacherous, graded mountain road and a grinding, long stretch of freeway, usually a trip of more than ninety minutes.

For Carol, not being there was the most bitter part. "I fantasized that if I'd been home, I could have somehow stopped the fire," she mused sadly. "I've been tortured by not having been there and the thought of what I could have taken from the house."

Karen McClung had gone early to play with her soccer team in a game out in Castro Valley, southeast of Berkeley. "I had no idea about the fire until I was on the freeway coming back," said Karen. Finding her normal freeway exit closed, Karen looped around through downtown Oakland and tried to make her way back on surface streets. She was stopped again by police barricades in the Rockridge district of north Oakland. She drove to a friend's house where she abandoned her car and started on foot toward Berkeley. "I parked my car and started running. I got to the underpass under Highway 24 by Chabot School and I stopped. All I could see was smoke. I couldn't tell where anyone was. I must have stood there for about an hour."

Karen unwittingly had headed right into the path the fire took in its fierce initial drive down the ridgeline and across the freeway near Chabot Road. Cut off from contact with her husband and children, with no idea how to reach them, Karen was surprised when out of the gloom emerged the fourteen-year-old son of some friends. "Nathaniel was separated from his parents and a cop asked me if I would take him," said Karen. Together they walked to another friend's house in the neighborhood to use the phone. Telephone service was erratic during the disaster, with some lines out and the remaining ones jammed. "It occurred to me to call my parents in Sacramento, since I was having trouble finding the number of the place where Nathaniel's family was," said Karen. "It was such a relief because they had heard from both of my kids and knew where they were, and they were able to get me the unlisted number of the house where I could reach Nathaniel's parents."

Families and Heroes

Families that went through the fire together emerged from the extraordinary experience closer and with a heightened sense of appreciation for one another.

When Jeff Grote said, "They are my heroes," referring to his daughters, he was echoing the sentiment of many parents. The teenagers that day often seemed to display more pragmatism than the adults when faced with evacuation.

Shelley Nan's account of the fire is a tribute to her children. Shelley, a concert pianist, and her husband, Sam Tabachnik, lived in a house on Vicente, near the Kusmierskis'.

Shelley Nan: Our son Matti, who was seventeen at the time of the fire, was home with me. He is the one who evacuated us. He took video of the last twenty minutes. We knew the fire was so close. When he shot his room he said, "Good-bye to the best room there ever was."

Our son Azie was almost twenty. He was living in his fraternity house at Cal—just five minutes from home. They had to evacuate from the frat house too. He felt it was important to be with us during the fire. A lot of his things were at home since he lived so close, so they are all gone. He lost his tux.

Azie is the one who pulled us together after the fire. He said to us, "Stop being a victim. Turn it around. Either buy or rent a house." We were the first family that bought a new house—within twenty-four hours of the fire. I attribute that to my son. He forced us to cope. He did not let us fall apart.

Then, a couple of weeks after the fire, he called and asked, "How are you and Dad doing?" I said, "Fine." Azie said, "Good, because I'm falling apart." He took a couple of weeks off from school. He's okay now.

Our daughter, Aviva, was the most balanced, carefree eight-year-old. After the fire, she wore only black for months. She didn't know it was the color of grieving.

She made a picture for us two days after the fire. It is a heart that says in the middle, "Love Together." It's surrounded by flames, but she said, "Those aren't flames."

As a family we reaffirmed our love and commitment to one another.

Aviva Tabachnik's best friend is Sarah Lesser, age nine. The Lesser family had the oldest house in the neighborhood, a 1909 George Plowman Craftsman, where they had lived for two months short of twenty years when it burned to the ground. No one in the family was at home when the fire started. Sarah and her sisters, Rebecca, eleven, and Hannah, five-going-on-six, were in Sunday school at Temple Beth Israel in Oakland. Their father, Michael, was on his way in the family van to pick them up. Their mother, Debbie, was teaching Hebrew at a synagogue in Marin County, across the bay and north of San Francisco.

Older brother Eli, who was nearly twenty, was away at college at Georgetown University in Washington, D.C.

Sarah: We were in Hebrew school. The kids were all watching the fire. You would see little red flames in the smoke, then a big spark. We thought it was our house that was going up.

Rebecca: There were two minutes of class left and a boy went outside and said, "There's a humongous black cloud."

Hannah: We found a black cloud with the teacher. We thought it was a rain cloud, but it was really smoke.

Rebecca: Dad picked us up. It was really dark, with this black, gloomy cloud hanging over. When we got to Domingo we were more and more worried: why had they blocked off the road? There were all these cars coming down Tunnel Road. Dad said he was going to try to go up to our house. We have friends who live across the street from the Claremont Hotel. Dad said, "I'm leaving you with them." They were loading their cars, so we helped them.

   We packed their precious stuff. In a cabinet I found the decoration from the top of the cake when they got married. So I put it in a bag. The next day, when they were unpacking, the husband gave the wife a kiss, because he thought she had remembered to take it.

   Hannah remembers this incident differently.

Hannah: I said, "Take this," and they let me take the little bride and groom into the car.

Rebecca: You could hear explosions. Every so often you'd hear *boom*. You'd think: that's my house. But it would be a transformer.

Sarah: Dad came back down just at the moment we were getting in the cars to leave. He looked sort of funny: he was riding my sister's bike and carrying his briefcase in one hand. He also had this valuable painting under his arm and he was wearing a straw hat. Grandma called later and said she saw him on CNN.

When Debbie Lesser left home before eight o'clock that morning to teach Sunday School in Marin County, she said everything seemed normal, "except for a strange, very dry wind." Heading back toward the East Bay at about twelve-thirty, she was startled to see "an incredible gray cloud streaked with yellow and black" in the sky to the south.

Debbie Lesser: I turned on the radio in the car. The news said there was a fire around the Caldecott Tunnel. At first it didn't dawn on me that it would be near us. Driving back I felt the adrenaline rush from being separated from my family.

Debbie's anxiety was heightened when her regular freeway exit was blocked. She finally made her way on surface streets into Berkeley and parked her car on the west side of Tunnel Road.

Debbie Lesser: When I parked the car I saw a friend on a bike. He said there was fire in his backyard at Tunnel and Bridge Road, near Alvarado, and that everyone had evacuated. I went to the house of some other friends and found them getting ready to evacuate. I used their phone and called the house. No one answered, so I tried my husband's office, which was nearby.

There was no answer, but I thought the family might be heading there so I got back in the car to go over. As I was driving I stopped to talk to another friend, whom I saw in the street. Suddenly, along came my husband in the van. He said, "I've got the painting!" I said, "Great, what about the kids?"

It was like a miracle that I found him. Within five minutes he said, "I'm going back up." I said, "No, you're not!" We decided I would go and be with the kids and he would go back to see about the house. He didn't come back for one and a half hours. We were very uneasy. He stayed and helped a friend's son water down their house. That house survived.

I don't even remember what the streets looked like. I must have been in a sort of shock. Somehow, I got to the store and had a reunion with the kids.

The friends who evacuated the Lesser children took them to the store they own. A kids' emporium, the store specializes in children's clothing, toys, and furniture, all arrayed in one giant space. From this safe haven in Emeryville, at the far western edge of the Berkeley-Oakland border, the refugees could watch the fire in the hills to the east.

Debbie Lesser: We felt very safe down there. The kids felt very nurtured and could play with the toys. There was this "anything you want" atmosphere, which I really didn't want to encourage. People would come in from the fire and watch it on the TV news. I used the phone to call our family on the East Coast. We had a view of the hills from there and could see red balls of fire moving around. We tried to figure out where they were. Into the evening we saw them moving southward. There was another family whose house had burned down. We were totally in shock. It was very unreal for me because I hadn't been there when the fire started.

Michael Lesser is a physician who writes books on nutritional medicine. Like many others that day, when faced with the stark reality of an incinerating fire bearing down on his house, he found himself propelled into action to save whatever he could.

Michael Lesser: The police had barricaded the streets. After I dropped the girls at our friends' and left the van there, I ran up Tunnel Road. I ran uphill like a young man, just bounding up.

It was quite a scene: people were evacuating; it was smoky, with cinders and embers flying everywhere. You could see the fire approaching, coming over the hill at a rapid clip.

I ran into the house. I thought about taking the hose up to the roof, but we had a very steep, peaked roof. I had it in mind that I must get this Paul Klee painting. My daughter, Rebecca, had said, "Get my bike, Dad." She had just gotten it for her birthday. So I wrapped the painting up in a shirt and got my cash, some documents, and one manuscript. I had three books in progress. I couldn't take anything else. I tried to turn off the gas, but couldn't do it myself. Gene Farb from across the street helped me. I got on the bike with the painting and my briefcase and rode out. Apparently I was on CNN like that.

I got back to our friends' house just as they were leaving with the girls. I got in the van. At this point I was looking for Debbie. It was amazing that I found her.

This time when I went back up to the house my mind had started to work. I wasn't so panicky. I ran past a fire truck at Tunnel and Bridge Road hosing down several houses. But when I got within three hundred feet of our house I saw I couldn't get any closer. The fire had already gotten to the red-wood tree in the front and the house was enveloped in black smoke. I couldn't see the house very well. It was pretty scary.

As I was standing there thinking maybe I can still get back inside, a friend of our son Eli's from high school appeared just like that. He said, "It's done for," and convinced me that I shouldn't go back in. The fire was coming from two different directions: down Alvarado and down Vicente. There weren't many people trying to fight it, just three or four volunteers.

The experience of fighting the fire produced both a clarity of focus and a distortion of reality. It was as if the intensity of the moment sharpened the strategic instincts but suppressed certain rational judgment.

Jeff Grote stayed to try to save his house on Vicente Road even after the firefighters left. Later he said he regretted not spending more time gathering things from inside the house. Others said they wished they had stayed longer to try to fight the fire. Although no one was killed in Berkeley, it remained a very real possibility throughout the height of the fire that a house could explode or ignite from radiant heat without prior contact from flame.

Jeff Grote: The fire was coming down the slope into our backyard. Every time you'd turn your back on it, it would come at you. The flame was like molten lava. The intense, hot air was like a giant convection oven.

All of a sudden the house two doors over exploded, with no flame nearby. Two redwoods up the street caught fire like matchsticks. A fire engine that had come up from Tunnel Road hooked to a hydrant and one of the firemen said, "Okay, you can help pull hoses." Another fireman joined me in the backyard. My greenhouse was going. I said, "Keep the redwood from going." He said, "If this tree goes, we drop the hose and run."

A Monterey pine in the back started to go. It had flames halfway up. Then the whole woodland behind us exploded and the fire flashed like napalm spreading. A fireball from one of the trees flew across the street and blew up the house there. The fireman said, "Oh, shit. Get down!" There were flaming boards, doors, and all kinds of stuff flying through the air.

At that point, the fire hose went off. Then another fireman walked up from Tunnel Road to tell the firemen with this engine to quit. "We're pulling out," he said. "The whole canyon up here is an inferno, it's a blast furnace."

There was a fifty-mile-per-hour wind blowing up the canyon. It seemed that it was sucking air in, keeping the heat at bay. I said, "We can save these houses. I still have plenty of water pressure from the garden hoses." The fireman told me, "I don't think we can save Berkeley."

I stayed longer. Dan Keuner, a Cal student who was renting a room from the Goetsches next door, had stayed with me to fight the fire. He was in the back of the houses with a hose and we were calling back and forth to each other. We also kept water on the house on the other side of me, and that house was saved.

It was like midnight, even though it was early afternoon. Once the Goetsches' house began to burn, we knew we had better get out of there. I remembered my wife's set of antique silverware was still in the house. When she left she had locked the door, and my car was parked down at Tunnel Road with the house keys in it. Dan said, "We shouldn't go in. The house could blow at any time." I grabbed a cobblestone, thinking I would break down the door and just run in fast. But I couldn't bring myself to smash the door because I had just installed it! I knew I was on the edge there, and that Jessie and the kids were probably worried.

Finally, I didn't go back in for the silver. I didn't smash the door. I just took a final picture of the house. Only Dan and I were there.

Conflagration

Holding the Line

The firefighters on Tunnel Road (near the junction of highways 13 and 24) were intensely involved battling the blaze that was roaring down toward them. Orth's strategy was to try to save the houses on the high side of Tunnel and to keep the fire from jumping the road and coming around behind his position. He knew the fire had crossed Tunnel farther up and feared that a pincer movement was already under way.

While Corrigan was still on Vicente, Orth and Dismuke, overwhelmed by the conflagration raging around them, had decided to move their command post back down Tunnel to the intersection with Bridge Road. "When I pulled our companies back, there was house-height fire flow," said Orth. "It was horizontal and downslope. The noise was an absolute roar. I told the guys: When it blows over us, get to the center of Tunnel Road by the concrete wall and try to keep your hoses going. We might have to pull out. We didn't want to pull out."

Engine 2 was located the farthest up Tunnel in the chain of hydrants and hoses established by Orth. As director of the whole operation, Orth had turned over command of the engine's firefighting activity to Shepard Lewis, who was on the rig with Ken Vallier and Robert Perez. Perez, an off-duty firefighter/

paramedic, had shown up at Station 2 earlier in the day and joined the engine company as an extra, fourth member. Now his presence allowed the engine to be fully staffed with its usual complement of three firefighters.

The Engine 4 company, Captain Ernie Jones, Apparatus Operator Bill Meilandt, and Firefighter George Huajardo, had set up on Tunnel Road and Vicente to fill the gap between Engine 2 and Engine 3. They ran lines up and down Tunnel to the burning houses and aimed the spray of the engine's deck gun to form a curtain of water to stop the fire from jumping across to the lower side of the road. Engine 4 also had a hose line up Vicente, helping to save the houses at the Tunnel Road end of that street.

"The wind was heavy," Orth recounted later. "Blowing embers and ash were spreading fire behind the line on Tunnel. Spot fires were flaring up in front of the line. Uphill from our position we were attacking these fires with the developed hose lines and deck guns."

Despite concentrated activity, the first two houses on Tunnel below Hiller were lost. The next house toward Vicente was saved, although its detached garage was destroyed by fire coming through the backyard. The house on the corner of Vicente was saved.

With Vicente Road completely engulfed in flames and the fire pressing down from both sides of Tunnel Road, Orth knew he had to make a defendable line. He also knew that houses had to be written off—common practice in wildland firefighting, where hundreds of uninhabited acres may be involved, but a hard realization for city firefighters accustomed to throwing all the resources necessary into the saving of one house. At the height of this fire, one house ignited every eleven seconds and there were never enough forces to stop it.

David Orth wrote in his report:

As I assessed the situation, I determined that we could hold Roble Road and Roble Court. I did not feel I could hold Vicente Road above Tunnel because the houses on Tunnel below Hiller were already fully engaged in fire. I also noted that there was fire behind my position on Tunnel, moving down toward Bridge and Alvarado. Requests were made for additional manpower and companies. But it was clear that help would be delayed.

"My one main priority," he said, "was to hold Tunnel Road to halt the spread of the fire further into Berkeley, and to keep access open. I was trying to save Berkeley, but I only had so many engines. Whenever I got reinforcements I split them between Roble and Tunnel. Once I violated common practice and split up a strike team, sending three engines to one side of Tunnel Road and two to the other.

"I formulated a plan to reposition the companies in what I felt would be a defendable line: Roble Court to Roble Road, to Tunnel, up on the low side of Tunnel as far as Vicente, and down Tunnel on the high side to Bridge, up Bridge to Alvarado.

"Once the line was in place it became offensive. And then we were able to save a number of houses in the area above Tunnel, bounded by Alvarado and Bridge, that earlier we had written off. At that point we were able to tie in to a line under Oakland's control going up Alvarado above the Claremont."

The Fight to Save the Claremont

When Corrigan's Engine 3 was pulled off Vicente Road, it was sent to fill in the line at Bridge Road and Alvarado. Bridge is a short street that connects Tunnel Road with one section of Alvarado. Off-duty Berkeley firefighters, recalled to duty throughout the afternoon, joined the engines already in place and later became relief crews. The fire had advanced down from both ends of Alvarado from Vicente on one side and from the ridgetop streets of Gravatt and Amito above the Claremont Hotel on the other.

Alvarado Road snakes back and forth as it climbs from Tunnel Road to the hill above the Claremont. Footpaths running straight up the hill—Willow Walk, Eucalyptus Path, and Sunset Trail—connect segments of the road. The houses that lie between the paths are hard to reach by vehicle and in many cases impossible to reach by fire engine.

Berkeley Fire Captain Ron Falstad, who joined Engine 3 in the afternoon, described the operation at Alvarado and Bridge in his written report:

> A Naval Air Station engine company was set up at the intersection of Bridge and Alvarado. The engine had numerous hand lines coming off of it and a deck gun that was shooting over the houses on Alvarado. The fire had burned right through the backyards of some of these homes, up to the structures. The deck gun operation did a great job of protection on three of the homes directly north of the intersection. There was another engine company set up at Alvarado, 50 to 100 yards toward Vicente. This left about four or five houses in between that were unprotected, so we directed our efforts on these.

Falstad and the crew were protecting houses whose yards backed on the houses that were already on fire, on the loop of Alvarado above.

Facing page: Firefighters massed to hold the line behind the Claremont Hotel, fearing that the venerable wood-frame structure could become a "conflagration breeder" if it caught fire. Photo by Wesley Wong, **Contra Costa Times.**

> The houses on the uphill side were fully involved. A wood-sided house, at the corner of Alvarado and Willow Walk, was starting to burn from the eaves and attic. We didn't have enough line to attack the fire there; we could only protect where we were. Fortunately, another company saw the structure and found a line to attack and extinguish the attic fire. This was a significant stop, since it freed us to concentrate on the spread of the fire from the structures up the hill. . . . Later our position was flanked on both sides by companies from the San Francisco Fire Department.

The Berkeley crews joined a full-blown effort involving firefighters from San Francisco and other cities, including Oakland, Piedmont, and Hayward, to stop the fire on the hillside before it could burn down to the Claremont Hotel. Built in 1915, the Claremont is one of the largest wood-frame buildings still standing in the United States. Its gleaming white facade rises to a roofline of

gabled windows, and then up to a towering cupola, making the building appear at once stately and quaint. The Claremont dominates the dark, wooded hillside behind it, gracefully recalling an earlier era. When firefighters considered the Claremont, they thought of another venerable structure in their collective firefighter memory: the old Sheraton Palace Hotel in downtown San Francisco. In the fire that burned San Francisco in the wake of the 1906 earthquake, that stately structure became known in fire jargon as a "conflagration breeder," its ample wood frame generating heat and flame to spread the fire far beyond its walls. "The decision to pour all the effort necessary into saving the Claremont was a strategic one to halt the fire from spreading into the flats and perhaps destroying all of Berkeley," said Berkeley Fire Chief Cates.

The fight for the Claremont was dominated by a San Francisco Fire Department strike team under the command of Battalion Chief Paul Tabacco. About eighty additional San Francisco firefighters who were unassigned to fire apparatus were bused to Berkeley with their equipment in one of the San Francisco Municipal Railway's double-articulated buses. The firefighting effort involved dragging hundreds of yards of hose lines up the steep footpaths to reach the inaccessible backyards that lie between the paths. The densely wooded yards created an unbroken fuel chain for the fire to travel through.

Although the Claremont lies just across the Berkeley city line in Oakland, by 2:00 P.M. the newly formed Unified Command, composed of the fire chiefs of Oakland, Berkeley, and the tiny town of Piedmont, had placed the Berkeley Fire Department in command of the area. Radio communication to Oakland had been fragmented, and this, the northern fire front, was isolated from Oakland's southern fire line. The change in command was largely a formality since fire crews from Oakland, Piedmont, Berkeley, and other cities, plus the large San Francisco contingent, were already on the fireground.

A problem that confounded firefighters in this area was the incompatibility of hydrant and hose couplings. Most present-day fire hydrants are standardized with two hose outlets: one that is four and a half inches in diameter and a smaller one of two and a half inches. On hydrants in Oakland, however, the smaller connection is two and seven-eighths inches. To make matters worse, many of the older Oakland hydrants in the hills above the Claremont have only the smaller outlet. Although Berkeley fire engines typically carry a set of adaptors because they frequently cross into Oakland to fight fires, none of the engines on the scene from other cities had such equipment.

Berkeley's Falstad encountered another example of obsolescence. He found hose lines lying abandoned that he couldn't get to connect to any other hose, even though they appeared to be the standard inch and a half for hand lines. Puzzling over this, Falstad realized that these lines carried the antique Pacific Coast thread that has since been replaced by National Standard thread. Pacific Coast thread is cut at a different angle, with a different number of threads than the modern standard. It dates from the days when San Francisco manufactured its own fire hose. Although West Coast fire departments have standardized their equipment to the national standard, Falstad believes that the old-style hose can still be found on standpipes of older buildings. He noticed that the nozzle was of a modern, anodized material and concluded it must be of recent manufacture. He decided that the hose was from a "standpipe pack" of hose carried on San Francisco fire engines for use at old apartment and commercial buildings, and must have been among the piles of equipment brought over from San Francisco to outfit the scores of firefighters who came on a Muni bus.

Between 5:00 and 6:00 P.M. the wind shifted direction, no longer blowing fire directly toward the Claremont. The firefighters eventually held the fire line along Eucalyptus Path and Alvarado, although spot fires continued to threaten individual structures far into the night. By morning it was clear that the fight for the Claremont was won. The landmark wooden structure that firefighters feared would turn into a giant torch and set the rest of Berkeley on fire was saved.

CDF Arrives

By about seven o'clock that evening the command hierarchy at the Unified Command post was notched up again, as the "overhead teams" from the California Department of Forestry (CDF) began to arrive. CDF, the state's wildland fire expert, also acts as a kind of administrative superstructure in dealing with major fires. For example, the responsibility for calling for mutual aid had passed from Oakland (the north county coordinator) to the Naval Air Station at Alameda (coordinator for the south county), then to the Lawrence Livermore Lab (the overall Alameda County coordinator), and then to CDF, which could call upon statewide resources. The CDF teams did not actually take over the administration, but—with experts in fire operations, plans, logistics, and finance—assisted in building the incident command structure.

Fire companies from all over California were staged at the Naval Air Station in Alameda. Photo by Jane Scherr.

"CDF had people who knew where to get portapotties, food, blankets, showers, cellular phones," said Fire Marshal Bard. "By this time there were about four hundred fire engines inbound from all over the state. There were going to be two to three thousand people running around. We needed a field kitchen that could serve nine thousand meals a day. CDF called up the Water

One firm in Redding, in northern California, and they sent down a big old water truck. When you took the sides off, there were forty showers. CDF's finance people helped us to keep track of how much everything was costing so each city could get reimbursed."

By late Monday morning the command post moved off the freeway and down to the Naval Air Station at Alameda. The rest and feeding area for the crews, as well as the equipment staging area, were also set up there, and Berkeley Fire Department's use of Berkeley High School as a base camp was discontinued.

Roble Road

On the southwest, or low, side of Tunnel Road, Orth's line of defense extended down Roble Road to Roble Court, where Lieutenant Charlie Miller, as part of the first-alarm response, had arrived at about 12:30 P.M. and established Roble Command. On Engine 5 with Miller were Firefighter Bruce Johnson and Driver Ace Adams. The mission on Roble was to try to protect the area from fire that was burning up from Chabot Canyon on one side and down from Tunnel on the other.

Roble Road and its spur, Roble Court, derive their name from the *roble,* the Spanish word for the live oak tree that grows densely there, along with California bay laurel and an occasional towering cedar. The road is lined with great sycamores, and every property is thickly planted with trees and shrubs, including magnolia, rhododendron, and olive. The trees made the firefighting effort difficult, often obscuring houses from view. Also, as the fire traveled through tree crowns, overhanging branches ignited houses at the rooflines.

The Roble neighborhood is established. The oldest houses, modified Tudor and Spanish Colonial Revival, date to the teens and twenties. Many of the residents count their tenancy in decades too. Helen Moncharsh had lived in the old McDuffie estate for forty years when the fire struck. Ruby and Bill Reade live in the house they built more than thirty-five years ago.

At the far end of Roble at Chabot Road in Oakland, the large, two-story Craftsman house designed by Bernard Maybeck, known as the Chick House for its original owner, stands alone amidst empty, burned-out lots. The house caught fire at the roofline but was saved by intensive firefighting efforts. Enormous oaks surround the house. Months after the fire it was ironic to see their fire-scorched, copper-colored foliage draping over the brand-new roof.

After the fire, every house at the Berkeley end of Roble was still standing, with extensive damage in only one and lesser damage in others. On El Camino Real, an adjacent road that runs from The Uplands to an end point near Chabot Road and the Oakland border, two houses were lost and several damaged. Berkeley's firefighting efforts had extended down Roble and had saved houses in Oakland, although the devastation on lower Roble and Chabot Road was fairly complete when the Berkeley forces arrived.

That most of the Roble neighborhood in Berkeley was saved was due in part to the dynamics of the fire and the terrain: Roble was on the fire's flank, not in its direct path, and is in an area that slopes away from Tunnel Road, so that the initial firestorm roaring down from Hiller Highlands blew overhead. But fire crews who battled on Roble for more than twelve hours found a persistent fire that flared up on all sides. Flying brands landed on roofs and ignited houses, and the dense foliage and overhanging trees concealed the fire while feeding and accelerating it.

Roble Command's Lieutenant Miller said that the initial firestorm sounded "like a jet airplane roaring over our heads. You could see chunks of swirling, burning material. It was very frightening. I've read accounts, gone to classes, and have been to a lot of frightening fires, mostly inside of buildings. In those cases you feel that you have control. But in this we did not have the control. It was all around us.

"We couldn't have saved the houses we did without the efforts of the fire companies there and all the civilians who assisted," Miller went on. "When we got there we put out fires burning on eaves or roofs. We saved others that were already preheated and threatened by exposure to houses on fire next door. The fire had burned up the garden of one house and was so hot it had broken the glass of the windows, but we got in there and put it out. The area we saved is like a little finger extending into the destruction. It's the result of a tremendous effort."

Part of the second-alarm response to Roble Command was Fire Truck 2, with its crew of Lieutenant John Anderson and Apparatus Operators George Fisher and Randy Olson. The distinction between a fire truck and a fire engine is specific. An engine, originally known as a pumping engine, is about thirty-two feet long. An engine carries water and hose; a truck doesn't. A truck is actually the long "hook-and-ladder" vehicle of children's story books. It carries the equipment for entering and tearing apart a burning building: ladders and "hooks." Because of the nature of a fire truck, Anderson and Fisher needed to join forces with an engine company or borrow hose and hook it to a water source. Moreover, the narrowness of Roble Road and Roble Court made maneuvering the fifty-foot-long truck nearly impossible. So once there, Anderson and Fisher set off on foot to attack house fires and later to carry out reconnaissance. Olson was assigned to work with the crew of Engine 6, Firefighter Fred Ogleton and Apparatus Operator Bill Wigmore, under Lieutenant Neil Lochhead. Anderson and Fisher recalled that day:

John Anderson: When we responded to the second alarm at about 12:30, we saw heavy smoke and fire going across Tunnel Road. There was fire on three sides. It was really dark. We practically had to use our flashlights. It was very windy and there was lots of stuff in the air. Everything was on fire, everywhere you looked. It was like walking on a barbecue, there were coals everywhere. You could see this huge column of smoke.

George Fisher: There was boiling, black smoke. It was chaotic. People were going the wrong way on Tunnel Road: civilians fleeing, the press going up. The fire there was so hit-and-miss. You would see fire burning on a fence post but nowhere else.

Anderson: Initially when we were going up to the scene, I was really nervous. When we got up to Roble Road and Tunnel it was a pretty scary situation. I mean my throat was dry. When we first encountered Engine 5 and began advancing hose lines, there was wind and fire all around and we weren't sure if the fire was going to be able to surround us.

Fisher: I was exceedingly nervous on the way up there too. We had visions of getting caught in there. We didn't do the right thing, we drove the truck in head first. Later, we had to back it out. It was scary. It was so dark I pulled out a flashlight to lay lines. It was as dark as night even though it was noon. Streetlights were on. It was incredible. Neither one of us had ever seen anything like that. The sun was obliterated.

   We were concerned about getting overrun, and maybe we were discussing what we learned in our wildland firefighting class. It was hot and hard to breathe a lot of the time. It was so windy. Then the wind would shift. You could go in and out of areas where you could get small breaths of fresh air.

   Lieutenant Miller sent Anderson and Fisher down the road on foot into Oakland to investigate the extent of the fire. The pair returned with the news that the fire on lower Roble was burning its way toward them.

Anderson: You could see fire burning up from Chabot toward Roble Court, sweeping toward Berkeley. We were on the side as the fire blew through. We were dealing with the flank of a fire still burning. We were trying to protect houses on Roble and to keep the fire from advancing up to Tunnel Road. With the help of civilians, George and I advanced a line off Engine 5 down into the Chabot area. We were in Oakland practically the whole time. There were five or six houses threatened. We decided to make a stand at an old farmhouse on lower Roble that dates from 1874 and try to defend the unburned houses.

Fisher: We had quite a bit of civilian help on Roble Road, young college-age kids. We gave them short lessons in firefighting because we really needed the help. At the 1874 farmhouse, one of the first houses in the area, we handed two of those kids a hose line and said, "This house is yours. Knock down what you can."

Anderson: They were wearing T-shirts and I think one was in shorts. The house directly next door was fully involved and the garage was on fire. There was fire on every side. We ended up putting these two civilians between the unburned house and the exposure fire. It was smoky and dark and windy. The conditions were really tough. It actually got too hot for us and we had to go around the corner. And we had turnout coats and helmets on. We came back a couple of minutes later and they were still there with that nozzle, yelling and screaming and pouring water on, and they ended up saving that house.

Fisher: They did a tremendous job.

Anderson: Lieutenant Miller asked if anyone would volunteer to make an interior attack on a house on Roble Court. The second story was on fire. George and I volunteered with an Albany engine to put the fire out.

Then we continued on foot to see if there were any houses we could save. There were numbers of houses on fire. It was very windy.

One house at Roble Road and Chabot—we since found out that it's a Maybeck—was just starting to catch fire under the eaves and on the shingles from exposure to the houses on fire all around it. So we called and got the Emeryville engine down there to help. It was a unique firefighting opportunity, saving that house.

Fisher: The Emeryville engine ended up catching a hydrant that was in Oakland and laid lines down to us. We laid lines off their rig and made an attack on that home. There was a kind of balcony-type affair on the second story. A young civilian ran and did a pull-up and pulled himself up on that balcony. I tossed the hose up there and he put the fire out on the eaves of that home. Meantime, I took the easy route. I went inside and up the stairs and met him in the second-story bedroom and we put the fire out on the inside there.

As we left that home, we went in the people's refrigerator and had a cou-

Above: Anderson and
Fisher saw a bright, hot
fire coming from the
garage of this house,
where a car was en-
gulfed in flames. Most
of the houses on lower
Roble Road were fully
involved in fire when
fire crews arrived. Photo
by John Anderson.

Right: Anderson and
Fisher made a stand at
this 1874 farmhouse.
Photo by John
Anderson.

ple of sodas and gave some to the Emeryville firemen outside and I think there was a Hayward rig there besides. I left a note there that we had gone into the people's refrigerator and that we were sorry we had, but we did have something to drink and we appreciated it, and we signed, the Berkeley Fire Department. Several days later I went back up there and ran into the man that owned that house and told him I was the one who had taken the drinks from his refrigerator. He said that he still had the note and it was very meaningful to him and he would save it forever.

Anderson: After the Maybeck house we kept walking further into Oakland to see what we could find. Most had burned to the ground.

We came across this one Spanish-style house. Houses on both sides had burned down, and heat exposure had caught this one on fire. A fire company was there in a grass rig. These guys were out of water. So we got in there and

Fire from this house threatened the farmhouse next door (facing page). Two college-age volunteers helped Anderson and Fisher protect the unburned farmhouse from the exposure fire. Photo by John Anderson.

started helping them. We called for a couple more engines. We ended up saving that house. I have a picture of George chopping tiles on the roof of that Spanish house.

Fisher: About a month after the fire there was a party given for us by the neighbors in one of the big houses on Roble Road. We ran into the woman who owned the Spanish-style house there. We showed her a picture of us giving water to her cat. She was very grateful, not only that we had saved her house, but that her old tomcat had survived.

Anderson: At one Roble Road house that was obscured by trees we saw a guy who was trying to keep the fire from the house. It was real dark, and fire was burning in the trees. The front door was locked, so he picked up a piece of lawn furniture and crashed it through the window on the door. I ran down there and

The historic Chick House, designed by Bernard Maybeck, had just caught fire at the eaves when Berkeley firefighters arrived, saving the house. Its windows reflected the fire of a burning house nearby, giving the appearance of fire inside. Note drops of water from fire hoses splashed on the camera lens. Photo by John Anderson.

it didn't look like a house we could save. We only had a couple of hose lines. The man had a garden hose. He turned out not to be the owner, but somebody who was passing by, trying to save the house. I said, "Stay as long as you can, but when it gets bad, I want you to get out," because I was really concerned with his safety. We kind of forgot about him. We knew he was over there. We could see that fire was burning in the general area of the house. Sometime later in the fire, when things had calmed down, we came back to check on him. He was still there with the garden hose, but the fire was within ten feet of the house, pretty much on three sides of it. We were able to get an engine company down there, the Number 6 Engine, and we laid lines and advanced them up to the house. By the time we got water in those lines the fire was within two feet of the house, all the way around it. We ended up being able to save that house, largely because of that civilian who had stayed there during a big part of the fire.

Fisher: We had a young man approach us and ask us for a chainsaw. Ordinarily, we wouldn't be giving our equipment off the truck, it's just not the way we

Tremendous radiant heat from this burning structure threatened the Maybeck house nearby. Photo by John Anderson.

Above: *Fisher climbed out onto the tile roof of a Spanish-style house after putting out the fire in the upstairs bedroom. His efforts saved the house. Photo by John Anderson.*

Right: *One of the things firefighters do best: Fisher comforts the cat whose house he has just saved. Photo by John Anderson.*

operate. But the day was a little bit different than most. He pulled out his wallet and showed us his ID that said he was a tree cutter. What this young man did was go down Roble Road and drop trees that were creating exposure problems around a particular house. I'd forgotten about him until a couple of hours later. When we came back up through there, we saw a number of trees and brush that had been cut around this house, and the house was still standing. He had done an excellent job in removing the exposure problems. And just as we had instructed him, the saw was sitting there right where he'd left it. We picked it up and returned it to our rig.

Roble Road narrows to a tree-canopied tunnel. Hose lines were led off the engine and dragged up driveways to reach burning houses. Photo by John Anderson.

The Roble crew encountered citizen volunteers fighting the fire who appeared, seemingly, from nowhere and stayed at their posts, making the difference between saving a house and losing it.

Charlie Miller: We couldn't have had the success we did without civilians. They were the ones who said, "Hey, it's coming up behind you." It was a civilian, Fred Johnson, who told us the fire had come around to Roble Court and had started burning one of the houses. If we hadn't saved that house, all the others around it might have gone too.

If I said I needed a hose line moved, gee, you had to hold them back. A fully charged hose line is really heavy, but they would just grab it. With Anderson and Fisher some civilians pulled a three-inch hose line off the back of Engine 5 and dragged it 750 feet! By ourselves we could only have taken it about 250 feet, but they got it to where it needed to go. I had set up Engine 5 just below the split of Roble Court, as far down Roble as I felt I could go safely. Below us the road divided and got narrow. It looked like a tree-canopied tunnel, sloping downhill. I didn't want us to be trapped. But from that position, the volunteers dragged hose down to attack some of those burning houses in Oakland.

Fred Johnson, Jr., Julian Whitacker, and Cameron Johnson, as well as others who went unidentified, are to be commended for their bravery, insight, ability, and willingness to follow directions.

Fred Johnson kept showing up at just the right time with information and assistance throughout the action. Because of the large number of civilians who fought the fire shoulder-to-shoulder with us we accomplished things that we couldn't have by ourselves given our manpower. We've sustained cutbacks over the years in the fire department that have closed fire stations and reduced the company on an engine from four to three. Those reductions sometimes have caused delays.

Fred Johnson, Jr., is a young man in his twenties who was helping his parents evacuate the family home at the corner of Roble Court and Roble Road when Engine 5 came down the road. Johnson stayed at the fire all night, guid-

Six weeks after the fire the Roble neighbors invited the firefighters from Berkeley, Albany, Emeryville, and the Lawrence Berkeley Laboratory who had saved the neighborhood to come to a party in their honor. That sociable Sunday afternoon was a reunion for the residents and firefighters who literally had been through a trial by fire together. Here, Apparatus Operator George Fisher (left) and Captain David Orth (center) reminisce with residents about the day of the fire. Photo by Jane Scherr.

ing fire crews to "hot spots." He never left the neighborhood, but camped out in his house for several days, watching for looters as well as for fire, until his parents were able to get through police lines back into the neighborhood.

When Lieutenant Debra Pryor relieved Charlie Miller as the Roble Command Officer at around ten o'clock that night, it was Fred Johnson's door she knocked on to ask the location of a house where a new spot fire had been reported.

Pryor was Berkeley's first female firefighter when she joined as one of a dozen recruits eight years ago. The number of women in the Berkeley Fire Department has grown to seven, with one more on the current eligibility list. What the department's females lack in number they appear to have made up for in respect.

"I'm one of Deby's biggest fans," said Miller. "She was my backup commander and assisted me with her good judgment and energy as soon as she got there. She is an excellent firefighter and is doing a wonderful job as an officer. She also disproves any stereotypes that females don't have physical strength."

Volunteers played a major role in defending houses along the same fire front just one block down Tunnel on The Uplands and the streets that run off it: El Camino Real, Hillcrest Road, and Roanoke Road. On El Camino, during a fierce wind-driven attack of fire, about twenty civilians grabbed hand lines off Engine 7 to work with the crew: Lieutenant Gene Smith, Apparatus Operator Kim Larsen, and Firefighter Charles Morris. At one point, when the fire roared

Volunteers were an essential part of the firefighting force. Here they handle high-pressure hose lines on El Camino Real. The T-shirts and shorts worn by most of the civilians offered scant protection from the intense fire. Photo by Tom Levy, San Francisco Chronicle.

through, the crew had to abandon their positions to take cover, leaving the fire engine with its five-inch-diameter supply line still hooked to a hydrant. After the wind changed, they came back and found the engine still functioning. Volunteers also helped the crew of reserve Engine 11, led by Lieutenant Michael Nagamoto, to stretch hand lines along The Uplands from Hillcrest to El Camino. Despite an additional engine from the Lawrence Berkeley Lab fire department, there would not have been enough firefighters to hold the line without those volunteers, said Engine 7's Gene Smith. In the end, two Berkeley houses were lost and three more damaged. That many more were saved was the result of a concentration of people, effort, and determination, said Smith.

View of the Apocalypse

By evening the fire crews were "mopping up" on Roble Road. "Personnel were shifted and companies were released," wrote Charlie Miller, "but the release of companies in no way indicated a lack of need in the Roble area. Gas services were flaring and small fires existed throughout the area." Miller released crews for rest or reassigned them to other parts of the fire operation.

Fire Truck 2, with a crew of five, including Lieutenant John Anderson as its officer and George Fisher, headed up to Tunnel and Vicente, where an interior attack was needed on the home of Jim and Priscilla Troy, a former carriage house designed by John Hudson Thomas for his 1913 Wintermute mansion.

George Fisher: The house was back from the street on a long driveway, and the place was on fire upstairs. It was real smoky. There was a whole bunch of firefighters there with wildland gear—brush jackets—but no masks for smoke, and they needed a ladder. We carried a ladder from where we had parked the truck on Tunnel up Vicente to the house. The place was going good from the inside out, but we deemed it savable by virtue of our training in structural attacks. In our Berkeley firefighting training most of what we do is structural.

We got some masks, and Randy Olson and I went inside and made an interior attack.

John Anderson: I went around the back, up the hill, to check on Bentley School on Hiller Drive. It was a pretty good-sized place, consisting of a cluster of five or six buildings. Nobody was up there. It was on fire in the middle and the sides. There were fires all around it. We called the comm center and requested more help.

Bentley School, located on Hiller Drive in Oakland, just off Tunnel Road, was partially destroyed by the fire. Photo by John Anderson.

Fisher: When Lieutenant Anderson arrived back after checking Bentley School, he was *very* concerned for our safety because there were two of us in that burning house with no communications, no radio, and this place was going real good. He came in as far as he could downstairs and started yelling at us and told us to get the heck out. But I think we did a lot of good upstairs before we left. We knocked the fire down and the people who were fighting it outside finished

it off and eventually saved a majority of it. When I got out I threw the mask on the ground and we went up to Bentley School.

Anderson: We only got one engine company and some firefighters from Berkeley and LBL [Lawrence Berkeley Laboratory] to respond to Bentley School. All the exterior buildings were on fire. We fought there for a couple of hours and eventually were able to save the most historic building on the grounds. We stayed there for quite a while, until it got dark. We were so tired then. We lay down, sucking on oxygen.

Fisher: I was awfully hungry. I realized I had lost my ax at the last house we saved. When I walked back to get it I found a soggy pizza on the ground. I took it back up to Bentley School. There was a ladder on the brick building. We climbed up and lay down on top of it and looked out and ate that pizza.

After that we took the truck down the hill and stopped at Staging, at the

"Normally, the fire at Bentley School would have been a third alarm—seven engine companies and two trucks," said Lieutenant John Anderson. "But we put it out with a bunch of tired firefighters and one engine company." Here, hose lines are led off the Lawrence Berkeley Lab engine to save the school. Photo by John Anderson.

bottom of Tunnel Road. There were loads and loads of guys there who wanted a break, so we took seventeen or eighteen of them on the truck to the rest area at Berkeley High School.

Anderson: As we drove down Ashby to go to Berkeley High School, there were hundreds of people lining the streets and clapping as we went by. It felt like we were coming out of a war zone.

Fisher: We rested for about an hour and then went back out to recon the hill area above Claremont.

Anderson: I got permission to go up. I knew the area real well; I had grown up in that part of the Oakland hills above the Claremont Hotel. We were sent up with the Albany crew and rig, six of us altogether. I was the lieutenant.

When we drove up the fire was basically out. The operation of dragging hose lines up the paths above the Claremont was over. We met other companies, including some Berkeley firefighters, who had made a stand at Gravatt and Alvarado. We were in radio contact and able to call in companies where they were needed. At one point we put out an exposure fire in a house on Alvarado, close to the Oakland-Berkeley line.

We followed Gravatt all the way up, to my old neighborhood. My parents' house was in the fire area and I was wondering if it had survived the fire. They had since moved, but they had built that house. We ended up getting as close as we could, with the downed wires and all, and then walking the rest of the way. It was real scary. We thought the wires that had fallen might be live. I walked up to within sight of where my parents' house had been. As it turned out, the fire had burned down the entire neighborhood. It was a pretty strange feeling to see the area that I grew up in as a kid: the whole hillside and all the various houses, burned to the ground.

We pulled the rig over in a driveway on Gravatt. You could feel the heat on the cement. The spot overlooked Grandview and the whole Vicente canyon

Apparatus Operator Tao Takaoka and Firefighter Richard Ellison take a break at the rest area set up on the lawn at Berkeley High School. Photo by John Anderson.

*Smoldering foun-
dations and charred
shells of cars were all
that were left of the
Alvarado and
Gravatt Drive
neighborhood. Photo
by John Anderson.*

area. We got out of the rig and just stood there and looked out. You could see in the distance the rubble of houses still burning. It was like you were witnessing the end of civilization.

It was a very strange feeling. We knew we were probably one of the first companies to get up on that scene. It looked like an atomic bomb had exploded. There was a fine coat of ash on the streets and there were just chimneys standing and gas fires going. It was about two o'clock in the morning and it was dark because there were no streetlights and just these distant fires burning. We just stood there and were real quiet. We knew we were part of history, and we had fought this huge fire.

Flares in the Night

Intense fireground activity in the entire fire area had continued throughout the day, as flare-ups continued to be a danger from still-smoldering ruins. By the time of maximum fire spread, about five in the afternoon, the conflagration had stretched southward across Highway 24, deep into Oakland's densely built, wooded hill neighborhoods to the southeast and all the way to Claremont Canyon on the north.

It was only when the wind shifted and began blowing out of the west at about five o'clock that firefighters gained what they called "perimeter control" of the fire. But although the edges of the fire area did not expand much after that, isolated fires within the perimeter continued to burn into the night.

The phenomenon of "burn-back" or "infill burning" continued to claim houses and threaten others long afterward: fire that had flashed across un-burned areas, to create a new perimeter, then began creeping back.

One eerie and sad example of a house lost this way had stood high in the Oakland hills. As the fire progressed through the afternoon on Sunday, the house was clearly visible from the flatlands of both Berkeley and Oakland. People assembled on rooftops to watch the fire marveled at how that house contin-ued to stand as others around it were incinerated. Then, at about ten o'clock, as the burn-back phenomenon finally caught up with it, it went up like a torch and was consumed. With live electrical wires down and fire all around it, access by fire equipment was impossible, the fire departments said.

History of Fire in the East Bay

A PATTERN REPEATS ITSELF

The Berkeley Fire of 1923

In October 1991 Berkeley's architectural heritage was seriously diminished when more than sixty houses in the Claremont district, many dating from the beginning of the subdivision, were razed. One-of-a-kind designs by Maybeck, Coxhead, Gutterson, and Ratcliff were among those burned. These losses compounded the earlier loss of houses by some of the same architects in Berkeley's fire of 1923. That conflagration, one of the worst in modern record until the 1991 firestorm, leveled fifty square blocks just north of the university campus, burning 584 structures.

Walking today through the blocks burned in 1923 is like studying geologic history in rock strata and finding an entire layer missing. Evidence of habitation before 1923 is not apparent. Old photographs show that the neighborhood had been built with large, wood-frame houses. A block north of Cedar Street along Arch Street there is an abundance of Victorian and Craftsman houses dating from the 1880s through 1920, but once you cross Cedar into the immediate vicinity of the campus—on Hilgard, Virginia, and Euclid streets—the architecture abruptly switches to stucco bungalows and apartment buildings of the twenties, thirties, and forties.

Familiar Fire Conditions

On September 17, 1923, the same kind of hot, northeasterly wind that created the 1991 firestorm blew a grass fire out of a dry canyon and into one of the most densely developed neighborhoods in Berkeley. The fire had started the night before in Wildcat Canyon in the rugged hills to the east. Because the houses at that time did not reach as far up the hill, and were not built as close together as today, the fire traveled slowly, down through the dry grasses and brush, reaching Codornices Park above Euclid Street by about noon on the seventeenth.

People living along Euclid smelled smoke before they realized the danger they were in. The first fire call came in to the Berkeley Fire Department at 2:05 P.M. By 2:30 all of Berkeley's fire equipment was at the scene. The first attempts to save individual houses were abandoned when the fire jumped over firefighters' heads and raced on a thousand-foot-wide front through blocks of wood-shingled houses in the north campus neighborhood. The fire spread through Monterey pine and eucalyptus trees and lapped up wood-shake roofs as if they were its favorite food. The fire department tried to make a fire line, battling the wind-driven blaze with inadequate water supplies, in their attempt to halt the fire's spread. For the first two hours of the fire, calls to nearby cities were useless because neighboring fire departments were already occupied with other fires. Finally, late in the afternoon, the fire crews gained control of the fire when the northeasterly wind died down and gave way to the normal moisture-bearing westerly wind. The wind changed at about the same time as help arrived from other fire departments. The fire burned as far west as Shattuck Avenue and was stopped from moving south onto the university campus at Hearst Avenue. Firefighters at the time opined that if the wind hadn't changed, the conflagration might have burned all the way to the bay.

The comparison with October 1991 is obvious. There were the same "critical fire conditions": dried-out, late-summer vegetation turned to tinder by high temperatures and low humidity, and a dry, interior wind, which blew on an identical course as the wind of October 20. And in both cases the shift in the wind was a primary factor in bringing the fire under control.

The Berkeley fire of 1923 leveled fifty square blocks on the north side of the university campus. The house on the left, at the corner of Hearst and Arch, burned to the ground. It was the home of Frank Armstrong, great-grandfather of

Phil Gale of the Berkeley Historical Society. Armstrong's son, Jack, took this shot from across Hearst on the U.C. campus. Photo courtesy of Phil Gale, Berkeley Historical Society.

In the wake of both fires there was a sense of disbelief that an established residential area could be threatened by wildfire. The fire of 1923 was an early case of a wildland-urban fire. It must have been a shock to Berkeleyans that their neighborhood could be so vulnerable to what happened in the park land on the other side of the ridge. The degree to which the public now remains oblivious to the fire danger from adjacent wildlands will determine the level of preparedness for the future.

Lessons from 1923

The fire of 1923 resulted in an incredible awareness by the citizens of fire preparedness. Realizing that 92 percent of the buildings that burned had wood-shake roofs and that shakes were a great factor in spreading the fire, the Berkeley city council in 1923 immediately passed an ordinance banning any new wood-shake roofs. Although the wood-shake lobby succeeded in having the law rescinded after six months, a new awareness about building materials had taken hold in the public consciousness. Stucco houses with tile roofs replaced many houses that had burned down.

Architect Bernard Maybeck, whose north Berkeley home was destroyed in the fire, experimented with fire-resistant materials when he built himself a new home, which he called the "Bubblestone Studio." The construction method consisted of dipping burlap sacks into lightweight, pink-colored concrete and hanging them on wire framing while they were wet. The result, resembling sculpted shingles, did not catch on, although the whimsical cottage still stands in north Berkeley.

In the aftermath of the 1923 conflagration, the city's water system underwent extensive improvement. The East Bay Municipal Utility District was formed in 1923, consolidating various water and sewer services.

The 1923 fire destroyed a fire station in the hills, but three more were built in its place. The Berkeley Fire Department hired more firefighters and started regular fire patrols of the hills in the summer until the first rain. In fire season a full-time lookout was sent to a fire tower on Vollmer Peak, a 1,913-foot-high peak on the eastern edge of the park district that overlooks the dry open lands to the east.

Fire Preparedness

The Early Days

When Berkeley Fire Chief Cates joined the department in 1967, Berkeley still had ten fire stations, three of them located in the hills. Cates was first assigned to a firehouse high in the hills of north Berkeley. Now known as Station 7, it was then Station 10. "Fire protection for the hills was considered so important," recalled Cates, "that when the company went out, an engine from the flatlands would come up to take its place. Engine 10 would signal, 'Coming off the hill; stand by at La Loma and Cedar,' and the replacement would go to the top of Cedar Street, which is at the start of the hilly area." Eventually two of the three hill stations fell victim to budget cuts and were closed. Today the city has seven stations, one of them in the hills, and 130 firefighters instead of the 187 of twenty-five years ago.

In Cates's early years the fire department used an alarm and signal code tapped out on the Gamewell teletype to notify the stations of a fire, its location, the number of alarms, and which engines should respond. A loud warning bell called the "gong" sounded the alarm, and a lighter-toned bell known as the "joker" counted out the code. There were old-timers in the department who remembered the days of horse-drawn fire engines. The horses were stabled right in the firehouse. "When an alarm sounded the horses would step out of their stalls and stand and wait for the harness to drop down on them," said Cates, recalling the stories he'd heard. "The horses knew the codes so well that if the alarm was not for their district, they would stay in their stalls."

The lack of high technology in the early days was more than compensated by a hands-on familiarity with the fire operation by everyone: the fire alarm dispatchers, the firefighters, and the chiefs, not to mention the horses. Cates joined a fire department that was not suffering from the lack of public spending that hampers government services today. Fire engines carried four and sometimes five firefighters, instead of the three-person crew that is standard now due to budget cuts. Fire prevention efforts, such as burning overgrown brush on vacant lots and maintaining a fire outlook post in the hills, were fully staffed.

Forgotten Lessons, New Fires

Eventually the weather alert was discontinued, as was the fire lookout in the hills.

"The longer we got between 1923 and the present," said Cates, "the less sensitized the public was to the need for constant vigilance. The lessons from the '23 fire became less meaningful and the alert systems tapered off. There was no longer any significant fire experience in the public's memory.

"Finally, though," he said, "it snuck up and got us."

The Oakland Hills Fire of 1970: The Eucalyptus Controversy

In September 1970 fire struck the Oakland hills, burning thirty-seven houses. Then, after a freeze in the winter of 1972–73 left hundreds of eucalyptus trees dead in the hills, all the East Bay fire jurisdictions took a good look at the problem of combustible vegetation in the residential areas that face open park lands.

"The lesson of the 1970 Oakland hills fire was fuel management," said forestry expert Carl Wilson. On September 22, 1970, northeast winds whipped up a hot, fast-moving blaze in the same Oakland canyon where the October 1991 fire originated, burning through stands of Monterey pine and eucalyptus to destroy dozens of houses on Westmoorland Drive, Norfolk Road, and Marlborough Terrace. Many of the houses later rebuilt on those streets were burned down again in 1991.

But the urgency of the fire danger did not set in until two years later, when the freeze of December 1972 killed thousands of eucalyptus trees throughout northern California. Fearing that the dead trees would become a substantial fire hazard to the East Bay by the next fire season, a group of government and university forestry and wildfire experts, including Carl Wilson, formed a "eucalyptus team." They began a campaign in February 1973, with the fire departments of Berkeley, Oakland, Kensington, El Cerrito, and the East Bay Regional Parks District, to analyze the fire danger and spur public agencies into a massive eucalyptus removal and fuel-break program.

Eucalyptus, the tall Australian native with white, peeling bark, high crowns of drooping, narrow, blue-green leaves, and a distinct camphor or lemon aroma, had been introduced to California in the 1850s as a fast-growing hardwood source for railroad ties and construction. After thousands were planted, they were discovered to be unsuitable because the wood twisted and cracked in the curing process. So they remain, now part of the California landscape, growing in wind-break rows and large groves in which they are the dominant species.

Eucalyptus grows in great stands in the hills of the East Bay Regional Parks District. The freeze of 1972 killed about three thousand in the hills above Oakland and Berkeley alone. Because of their high oil content, the trees are considered flammable even when they are alive. Their habit of shedding prodigious loads of oily leaves and ribbons of loose, trailing bark creates a "fuel ladder" by which fire can be transmitted from the understory of dry vegetation on the ground, up chimneylike through the hanging bark, to the canopy of foliage above. When the trees are close together, the canopies can become the path for a crown fire that travels out of reach of fire hoses. The forestry experts studied reports from Australia of mass conflagrations occurring in huge eucalyptus forests there, propelled by flying firebrands of branches and bark.

The freeze-killed trees presented an even more serious problem, the eucalyptus team believed. Dried out but retaining their oil, the dead foliage and bark were especially explosive because those flammable oils were concentrated from lack of moisture. Foresters inspecting the dead and damaged trees noticed that the blue gum, the *Eucalyptus globulus,* did not drop its dry leaves, thereby resembling a torch waiting to be lit. The bark hung more loosely on the dead trees, exacerbating the chimney effect, and an increased amount of bark lit-tered the ground, which added to the fuel load of the understory. The less plen-tiful red gum, the *Eucalyptus camaldulensis,* tended to drop its leaves when dead, also adding to the dry understory.

But the concern over the eucalyptus generated controversy. Although it was generally characterized as a fire-spreading scourge, the tree had its defend-ers. Edward Stone, a forestry professor from the University of California, argued that the freeze-killed and damaged eucalyptus should be allowed to resprout. He cited cases of eucalyptus planted as fuel breaks in forests of more flammable trees, such as pines. Eucalyptus crowns are so high they generally are above the reach of fire on the ground, his theory goes. The fuel manage-ment programs should concentrate on all the flammable vegetation in an area, he argued, not just on the eucalyptus as the single culprit.

The eucalyptus fire hazard gained enough public attention in 1973 to result in hearings by the California legislature and a declaration of a state of emergency by the governor. The East Bay cities and open space districts with stands of dead eucalyptus began to clear out the dry accumulation of leaves, bark, and branches on the ground. Dead trees were cut and their stumps treat-ed with herbicide to prevent new sprouting. The eucalyptus team recommend-ed cutting a three-hundred-foot-wide, fifteen-mile-long fuel break along the wildland-urban interface. That year, work along a seven-mile stretch was begun, clearing entire groves in some areas and thinning trees in others.

In subsequent years, however, maintenance of the fuel break fell off. New accumulations of dry leaves and bark piled up on the ground. The scene was once again set for fire to move through the eucalyptus groves.

The Wildcat Canyon Fire of 1980

The next reminder of the deadly threat of wildland fire came in December 1980 when a grass fire started in Wildcat Canyon on Berkeley's northeastern border with the regional park. The fire ignited five houses in five minutes, burning them to the ground. The Berkeley Fire Department stopped the fire before it could do further damage, but the memory of the devastating 1923 fire was revived, since the origin and direction of the two fires were similar.

In the fire's aftermath, the East Bay Regional Parks District convened a "blue ribbon" panel of fire and forestry professionals, local government officials, and citizens to look at all the factors causing the wildland-urban fire threat and to recommend preventative measures. Their Blue Ribbon report, issued in early 1982, called for the cities along the park frontage to reduce the fuel load in the eucalyptus stands and grassy hills and to require strict clearance standards around houses. In response to the report, the Berkeley Fire Department declared a stretch of about 750 houses along the city's eastern boundary a "hazardous fire area" and initiated yearly inspections to enforce the clearing of combustible brush and the use of spark arrestors on chimneys.

State-of-the-Art Brush Clearing: Goats for Rent

Collapsible plastic fencing encircles a small herd of four-legged "fuel management specialists," chomping their way through a patch of blackberry bushes, Scotch broom, and poison oak. These days goats are a regular summertime sight in the dry hills of the East Bay Regional Parks District. They will nibble the long, dried-out grasses down to stubble before they are shunted out of this enclosure and into an adjoining one to start work on a new area.

The 1982 Blue Ribbon report on the Wildcat Canyon fire in Berkeley called for the extension of fuel breaks over the entire twenty-five miles of the park border as well as the clearing of existing breaks. Gary Bard and David Orth at that time were part of the Berkeley fire prevention team that coordinated the fuel-break program with Regional Parks and the University of California, made public presentations on the need to clear away flammable brush, and planned the Berkeley Fire Department's response to grass fires.

"We carried out exhaustive brush removal in the summer of 1982," recalled Orth. "Then that winter there was record rainfall. With the eucalyptus and chaparral that had held the soil gone, the rains set loose massive mudslides. The next summer we went back to the drawing board and hired goats."

Orth explained that there is a difference between a "down-to-the-dirt" fire break and a managed fuel break that seeks to control the height and density of vegetation. "In a managed fuel break you reduce the potential for flame height that is too high to control with hose lines. A bare-earth fire break that has accumulations of high chaparral on either side won't necessarily stop a wind-driven fire. The flame will jump across from fuel source to fuel source. Plus, if you pull out brush by the roots, you can have erosion problems.

"Goats are a great solution," Orth continued. "Not only are they cheaper than work crews with hand tools—they eat everything. They get rid of the fire hazard of the old, dried-out brush, but they leave the root structure. When the plant comes back, it's greener and therefore more fire resistant."

Freeze and Drought: A Recipe for Disaster

The winter of 1990 was unusually cold in the Bay Area. The climate is normally moderated by the Pacific Ocean, so that extremes in temperature are rare. When nighttime temperatures dropped below freezing in December, eucalyptus trees died. Their frost-scorched leaves hung on brittle branches, like so much tinder.

The following summer, in August 1991, Carl Wilson conducted a tour of the Marlborough Terrace neighborhood to demonstrate the hazardous fire conditions existing there because of combustible vegetation. His audience was a group of forestry and fire professionals, including fire chiefs from Berkeley, Oakland, the East Bay Regional Parks, and the California Office of Emergency Services. Visiting Australian foresters were also in the group. Wilson showed them the path of the 1970 fire and the deadly mix of frost-killed eucalyptus, Monterey pine, and dried-out grasses threatening the houses. The fact that the area had just recorded a fifth year of drought meant that the eucalyptus had already been weakened and that all the vegetation was in a bone-dry state.

"It's going to be a long, hot summer," Wilson told the group.

The Australians shook their heads at the gum trees and said, "This is the worst!"

No one knew that two months later history would repeat itself and Wilson's fire scenario would come true.

Wildfire and Grasslands

In October 1991, wildfire, as natural to California as the poppy, sprang out of the East Bay hills and claimed everything in its path. That the dry, grassy hills should catch on fire was not unusual. Fire is an integral part of the cycles of California's grass and brush lands and forests. That the fire spread to houses and, in igniting them, grew hotter—to conflagration proportions—turned a natural phenomenon into a human tragedy.

The conflagration was a classic case of the type of disastrous fire that is possible, if not probable, in the wildland-urban interface—the areas where single houses and subdivisions lie next to or encroach upon undeveloped wildlands. The old-fashioned urban conflagration, in which fire spreads from one building to the next, is largely a phenomenon of the past, since modern building codes are designed to make sure that fires starting in one structure are contained. But in a wildland-urban context the fire is already moving as a wildfire when it spreads to structures. Houses then add to the natural fuel load of vegetation, making a hotter and more destructive fire.

It is the wildland-urban fire that now poses the greatest danger to life and structures in the arid West, as development pushes into brushy hillsides or tree-filled canyons. Yet as people settle in these rustic areas, they are unaware of the neighbor with whom they share the wildland, one that has always dwelled there: wildfire.

Fire is one of the elements that shapes California's landscape. California's wild plant life actually depends on recurrent fire to regenerate it: some pine cones open only after a fire, and the seeds and corms of certain plants remain

Wildland Firefighting

When Tony Bacon lectures on wildland firefighting techniques he tells the class, "That's what's going to eat your lunch." A rising convection column that sucks up flaming debris and whirls it across your safety line to start new spot fires behind you; a fire in a box canyon where every side is burning and there is no way out; flames that race through treetops, generating more heat than you have water—that's what's going to eat your lunch.

"Fight fire aggressively but provide for safety first" is Bacon's primary rule. He stresses that saving life, starting with one's own, is the first priority on the fire line. "Sizing up a fire" is the key to smart firefighting. Rushing in without first assessing conditions can result in loss of life and loss of control of the fire. "If you don't know, don't go, may blow," quips Bacon. Fuel, weather, and topography are all factors to be evaluated when trying to assess how fast a wildfire will travel, how hot it will burn, and whether one has the resources to control it. Dense, dry vegetation, high temperatures with low humidity, and steep hills will speed up a fire's spread.

Bacon, who is a fire captain with the Novato Fire Department in the dry hills of Marin County, north of San Francisco Bay, teaches wildland firefighting classes under the auspices of the East Bay Regional Parks District. He also teaches under contract with the California Department of Forestry and the National Department of Forestry.

The summer following the disastrous East Bay hills fire was the second year Bacon presented his twelve-hour course to the Berkeley Fire Department. Firefighters from the adjacent cities of Albany and Emeryville and from the Lawrence Berkeley Laboratory on the U.C. campus also attended. Bacon gave the course to the Oakland Fire Department for the first time that summer.

Bacon tries to prepare urban fire departments, accustomed to the "static" situations of structure fires, to deal with the "dynamic" fire conditions of the wildland: shifting winds, a contiguous fuel (vegetation) supply, and a fire source that is not easily seen. The East Bay fire of 1991 was fought primarily by urban firefighters who lacked extensive wildland training, he says. When they were successful it was because they were employing wildland fire strategies, such as forming a defensive line for control of the fire's perimeter. Stories of wildfires often tell of vast areas burned before the fire is brought under control. If fire crews can make a defendable line and establish perimeter control at one point, they do so prepared to sacrifice the acres that lie between the head of the fire and their line. In the wilderness there are no structures to worry about. But bringing the same methods to bear in the wildland-urban intermix becomes a wrenching process.

"You must fight the fire as a wildland fire," instructs Bacon. "The toughest thing is to have to write off a house, but unless you have perimeter control you're going to lose more structures anyway."

Bacon notes that while a wood-shake roof and shingle siding put a house in a wildland setting severely at risk, in a worst-case fire scenario a tile roof and stucco walls can give a false sense of security. Tile-roofed houses caught fire in the October conflagration when pine needles accumulated under the tiles ignited. Stucco burned up in the intense heat.

What can make the critical difference is a well-groomed property where brush has been cleared away from a house and tree branches do not hang over a roof or chimney.

Access is another factor that determines whether a house can be saved. Narrow, winding roads will became clogged with vehicles trying to evacuate in a major fire, making passage for fire apparatus extremely difficult. Long, steep driveways and no backyard access can also isolate a house from potential help.

"An overgrown yard *and* a wood-shake roof *and* difficult access can add up to a death trap for a firefighter," Bacon says. "That may be the house you have to write off.

"We tend to place ourselves at greater risk in a battle to save homes than in a normal wildland fire. Don't forget *your* individual escape route. Back the engine down a narrow road or driveway, and know how you're going to get out if you have to cut and run."

dormant in the ground until fire releases them into life. California's first human inhabitants—the migratory Indians—understood the renewing property of fire and "managed" forests and grasslands with controlled burning. Later human response to fire has been to suppress it, to manage it, or to remain oblivious to it until it strikes.

Fire's presence is almost a constant, from natural causes and human ones. Fires in the wilderness start when lightning strikes dead tree limbs; when spontaneous combustion occurs in the tightly packed, decaying vegetable matter called "duff"; and when a rockslide tumbles flint and iron oxide together, creating sparks. People's activities also start wildfires: carelessness with cigarettes or campfires and deliberate incendiarism are major culprits. But a human being need not even be present: sunlight refracted from a partly filled bottle can start dried grass smoldering; exposed power lines falling to the ground or touching a dry branch can produce a dangerous spark; sparks from motor vehicles and construction or logging equipment can ignite roadside and forest fires.

California's Mediterranean climate creates conditions that are ideal for fire. The winter rainy season, from about November to March, produces vigorous growth in seasonal grasses. Summers are usually free of rain. So, during the six- or seven-month rainless stretch the uncultivated grass and brush lands turn tinder-dry. By the end of summer the official fire season arrives. In the fall the coastal areas may experience hot, dry winds blowing from the northeast, lowering humidity and further drying out vegetation. At these times wildland fire agencies declare red-flag alerts.

The Spanish and Yankee settlement of California, in the eighteenth and nineteenth centuries respectively, took place against the backdrop of this cyclical pattern of fire. Yankee mining towns of wood-frame houses sprang up and burned down repeatedly. The goal in a mining settlement was to put up a habitation swiftly, and any scrap lumber would do. Add to this the sparks from utilitarian fires—in stoves, chimneys, blacksmiths' forges—and the wildfires that lapped at the edges of the towns, and it is clear why these early communities were so vulnerable to fire.

San Francisco burned down six times in the eighteen months between Christmas Eve 1849 and June 1851, a half century before the earthquake and fire of April 1906 leveled the city. The city's rapid growth had started after gold was discovered in the Sierra Nevada foothills in 1848, and urgency rather than permanence was the criterion for building, as people poured into San Francisco on their way to the gold fields. Approximately twenty-eight thousand structures burned in the 1906 fire, most of them wood frame. So extensive was the flimsy wood construction that earlier in 1906 the National Board of Fire Underwriters had reported that "San Francisco has violated all underwriting traditions and precedents by not burning up" (Arthur E. Cote and Jim L. Linville, eds., *Fire Protection Handbook* [Quincy, Mass.: National Fire Protection Institute, 1991], p.6.140).

Since those days, cities have adopted modern building codes, which for the most part prevent those disastrous fires that wipe out blocks of cityscape. Such fires had been a threat to urban life since people first started living in cities thousands of years ago. The earliest fire codes aimed at regulating the causes of urban fires: clogged chimneys, wood or thatched roofs, open fires. The *Fire Protection Handbook* cites a fourteenth-century London regulation requiring chimneys to be built of stone, plaster, or tile instead of wood; it notes that in colonial Boston, despite a host of fire regulations, "fires were everyday occurrences" (ibid., p.6.140).

The first fire law in California was enacted by the Spanish and was aimed not at buildings but at fields. For the early Spanish Californios, who settled on large ranchos, the backbone of the economy was cattle. And the grazing lands so vital to that enterprise were also the lands the indigenous people traditionally harvested for grass seed and then burned to encourage regeneration of the seed. The Indians' livelihood came into direct conflict with that of the Spanish who, claiming the land for their use, suppressed and outlawed the burning practice. In 1793 Governor Arrillaga issued a proclamation that forbade setting fire to grazing lands.

The practice, which naturalist Henry T. Lewis discusses in his well-documented *Patterns of Indian Burning in California: Ecology and Ethnohistory*

(Menlo Park, Calif.: Ballena Press Anthropological Papers, 1973), of firing a stretch of grasslands at the end of the growing cycle, usually the end of summer, was an integral part of the Indians' management of their environment. The coastal Indians moved from shore to inland hills and valleys to Sierra foothills in an annual round of gathering seeds and acorns and catching fish and game. Setting fire to the spent grasses resulted in a more vigorous early growth with the first rains of winter. Depending on the type of plant—whether used for seeds and berries or for basket material—the "crop" was burned every one, two, or more years. Lewis describes how the burning regenerated not only the grasses but the entire ecosystem.

On California's coastal and inland hills, the grasses, chaparral brush, and trees grow in a "succession cycle." The first stage is marked by a balance between the herbaceous plants (grasses and flowers), chaparral, and widely spaced coast live oaks and California bay laurel. When eventually one species gains dominance and crowds out the others it is said to be at the "climax stage" of the succession cycle. By its nature, the climax stage maintains a status quo and does not include new growth.

Chaparral, the generic Spanish term for the dense, woody brush that grows on California's grassy hills, can include Scotch broom, coyote bush, chamise or "greasewood," manzanita, and scrub oak. The species in any particular area depends on climate, exposure, moisture, and soil. The succession of chaparral and the plants in its ecosystem is directly tied to the occurrence of fire. When chaparral reaches the mature or climax stage, dominating the area, it stops regenerating. It maintains its dominance not by new growth but by exuding a toxin into the soil that inhibits the germination of other species. In fact, at this stage, as it becomes drier and drier, chaparral is just waiting for fire. And when fire comes, it burns explosively. The old growth is burned, but the root structure remains. When the chaparral sprouts again, the resulting new growth is greener, moister, and more nutritious to foraging animals. The fire burns away the inhibiting toxins, and the plants lying dormant in the soil reappear. Some of the most abundant spring wildflower growth occurs in chaparral areas the year after a fire. A chaparral stand that has undergone fire is characterized by a greater variety of plants, more open area, and the return of browsing deer.

The tall annual grasses that cover the coastal hills, turning from green to brown in California's rainless summers, are for the most part not the grasses the Indian people tended. The grasses that prevail today are fast-growing annuals introduced from Europe for cattle grazing. This species attained dominance over the native perennials by virtue of its aggressive capture of water and its practice of releasing toxins. While the native grasses store some water for their use during the dry season, the European species utilize more water during their rapid green growth in the spring, then, dying, turn completely dry and brown in summer. Thus the perennials retain some fire resistance, but the annuals turn into what fire managers call "flash fuel," in stands two to three feet high. It is these flammable grasses that form the backdrop to the California suburbs built on the edge of open lands.

Controlled burning for forest management was out of favor during most of this century. The public consciousness that created the national park system one hundred years ago was a conservationist one. If forests were to be preserved, all fire was to be suppressed. The result was to disrupt the balance achieved by periodic fire. No longer did the coniferous forests of the Sierra Nevada grow in the open "parklike" stands described by naturalist John Muir in 1894. Instead, dead and dying trees, saplings, and mature specimens all competed for the same space, crowding each other and blocking sunlight. In the redwood forests, fire suppression slowed down the regeneration of young trees, which need space and sunlight. The cones on the giant sequoia can remain closed for twenty years, waiting for fire to open them. Periodic fires had encouraged a balance between species: favoring shade-loving incense cedar and fir during stretches between burns and, after fire cleared out an area, promoting the growth of pine seedlings.

Suppression of fire has created a huge buildup of dry understory in forests: fallen branches, pine needles, and leaves, as well as low-growing vegetation. When fire does occur it spreads through the accumulated fuels, climbs the understory into the tree crowns, and results in a far more devastating forest fire. A similar situation exists in brushlands. The longer the time between fires, the drier and more developed is the chaparral, which at its climax stage can be ignited like tinder.

Aftermath

DEVASTATION AND RECOVERY

Artifacts

The first thing that comes to mind is a graveyard. The charred hillside is barren, except for blackened trees and chimneys, that preside tombstonelike over burned-out plots. The chimneys stand, embarrassed, exposed, with their hearths jutting out in midair, at the edges of the scorched outlines that show where a house once stood.

On April 18, 1906, East Bay residents stood on the shore or on ferry boats and looked west to watch San Francisco burn in the aftermath of its big earthquake. The populations of Berkeley and Oakland burgeoned as people who were burned out in San Francisco built new homes and businesses in the East Bay. On October 20, 1991, San Franciscans looked east at the East Bay hills in flames and watched as a column of ballooning black smoke rose and gusted across the sky toward them.

The firestorm dropped ash on San Francisco. It dropped other things, too, swirled up in the updrafts and carried beyond the reaches of the flames. A woman in San Francisco picked up a singed cookbook page that had fluttered

Above: Exposed chimneys stood like sentinels over the fire-devastated landscape, their hearths jutting out in midair. Metal appliances were scorched beyond recognition, but sometimes an undamaged object, such as a teacup, would be found buried in the layers of ash. Photo by Jane Scherr.

Right: This jack-o-lantern marks the Halloween season amidst the ruins of a house. Photo © 1991 by Harold Adler.

Left: Foundation walls traced the outlines of hillside homes. Home-owners posted signs to try to protect their properties from looters or souvenir hunters. This property is in Oakland. Photo © 1991 Harold Adler.

Below: Nothing was left of cars incinerated in the two-thousand-degree fire but charred metal shells. This scene is of Hiller Highlands the day after the fire. Photo by Jane Scherr.

to the ground and wondered if it was the only remaining artifact from a life's accumulation.

The fire created overnight artifacts. It burned so intensely—a two-thousand-degree holocaust driven by raging winds—that houses suddenly were not there. Preheated by the radiant heat of the fires around them, houses would burst spontaneously into flames and be completely engulfed in fire in a matter of seconds. Other houses exploded. Homeowners sifting through the rubble and the yard-deep ash on their lots found evidence of this: objects wedged into foundations at the other side of the house from where they had been.

Homes became archaeological middens. What was surprising was how little actually was left. Metal appliances, scorched to the point of appearing rusted and smashed almost beyond recognition, spears of twisted rebar, fragments of charred beams, and shards of brick and tile looked like the work of a bomb blast. In the rubble was often the scorched shell of a car, flattened and stripped beyond the capacity of any junkyard, rubber tires and interior vaporized. Incongruities abounded. Digging through the layers of ash, one homeowner was amazed to find a teacup unscathed. At another property, a wrought-iron picket fence, twisted at right angles, hung down into the basement garage space like a ladder, crazily dangling a small appliance that might have been a dishwasher, impaled on one of its spikes. A gas meter had melted into grotesque contours, like the subject of a painting by Salvador Dali. A hole gaped on one side of the meter, like a nightmarish mouth.

Many of these hillside houses had been built at several elevations, either above or below street level. For those built on the high side of a street, the three concrete garage walls forming the bottom level were frequently the only definition of the house left. All the debris from the collapsed structure and the entire contents of the house had fallen there. The upper stories were outlined by the remains of foundation walls, arranged terracelike above. Houses that clung to the downward slope of a hill were marked by a walkway or sometimes a gate that had survived. But beyond the gate and the walkway everything vanished. The bare outlines of foundations slanted away from street level, inviting one to speculate what early civilization constructed these forms, and if, perhaps, they aligned with the sun.

The sense of home dies hard. In the week after the fire, these vestiges bristled with signs declaring: This Property Is Not Abandoned! One ironic owner had a No Vacancy sign tacked up in front of the bare lot. Pots of flowers and jack-o-lanterns for the Halloween season decorated foundation walls. Mourning residents returned daily or on weekends to sort through the remains, bringing lawn chairs and bottled water to make the places habitable. Often looters or souvenir hunters had gotten there before them. Objects valued by their owners only for having survived had been callously snatched. People were ambivalent about the weekend sightseers who cruised through the devastated neighborhoods. "Leave us alone!" was the feeling of many. Others understood that people cannot comprehend a catastrophe of this magnitude without witnessing it: the appalling landscape of ash.

Stories of Return

Coming Back

Early the next morning Jeff Grote returned to the scene of his desperate attempt to save his house.

Jeff Grote: I went on foot, climbing through the yards above the Claremont Hotel until I reached the blocks that had burned. It was startling to see the rubble. Everything was gone, down to foundations.

I came up Alvarado and around the bend to Vicente. Then I started running. When I came over the rise I looked for my house and it was gone! I was stunned. The fence along the neighbor's house was still smoldering, but their house was there.

I started sifting through the fine white ash and charred remains of our house. There was the silverware! But it was all a lump now. I found the front door knob, but the inside knob had been completely vaporized.

Then I found the most amazing thing: an unburned page from the book *Out of Africa*. I picked it up and began to read it. There was a description of someone who had left his house and returned, only to find it "no longer the perfect drawing." That seemed incredibly prophetic to me, since I had been planning and working on this house for so long. That's when I decided we needed a new "perfect drawing" and that I should get started on new house plans right away.

That afternoon I arranged for us to get an escort up there—the whole area was sealed off. The kids really wanted to see. It was as if we were visiting a grave site. The house had been the physical manifestation of our family's life.

A week later we came back. We took a brave picture of the four of us standing in front of the fireplace in the ruins, like one of those family holiday pictures. When we dug through the debris, it was extremely therapeutic: first to identify things and then throw them away. The only things that survived intact were the pottery pieces the kids had made when they were little. They mourned the loss of their childhood: the school pictures, the drawings. As a bulldozer was scraping off the debris, suddenly up through the ash floated one of those plaster hand prints one of the girls had made. It was eerie! When we pried open the dishwasher we found all the glasses had melted. The one thing that remained was a mug the girls had given me on Father's Day that said "Dad."

*Facing page, top: The ruins of the Grotes' house were still smoldering when the family went back the next day. Daughters (from left) Joscelyn and Alexandria, and their mother, Jessie, were stunned at the devastation. Photo by Jeff Grote. **Bottom:** Determined to build again, the Grote family struck a brave pose in front of the fireplace of their burned-down house. From left: Jeff, Alexandria, Jessie, and Joscelyn. Photo courtesy of Jeff and Jessie Grote.*

Guerrillas

The pull to return to one's house was strong enough to make law-abiding citizens evade police barricades.

Polly Armstrong: That night John wanted to go back to the house. I was really upset. I said, "I can buy a new house, but I can't buy a new husband." He said, "The wind has died down, it should be safe." He said he would just find a way. So he ended up doing guerrilla stuff, sneaking through backyards to get through the police barricades and back up to the house while I stayed at the hotel.

John Armstrong is a mild-mannered man whom one would not suspect of guerrilla activity.

John Armstrong: They didn't let me in anywhere. So I left the car and climbed the tennis court fences by the Claremont Hotel to get up into the neighborhood. In the end I must have climbed thirteen fences.

I met other men hiding in the bushes, trying to do the same thing. Tunnel Road was empty of traffic. All the lights were out, other than the light from the fire, flaring up and down Alvarado and Tunnel. There was no more commotion, all the people seemed to be gone.

There were fire trucks and hoses all over and water was everywhere, running down the streets and in the gutters. We've all seen fire, but the noise of the fire was something I had never heard before and never want to again. It was a roar, just like a jet engine. The sound pulsated and was interspersed by a series of dull explosions at constant intervals.

Standing on the roof at night, you could see fires inside houses through the windows. It was as if someone had turned the lights on, but it was a red glow. It was very creepy.

Polly: John stayed on the roof all night, putting out fires in our yard and in the neighbor's yard. There were a lot of men who came back or stayed to protect their houses. It was as if we had slipped back to the 1950s—there was no question that the women and children would evacuate.

Polly described how her husband found lengths of welded copper pipe from his carpenter supplies in the basement and used them to fashion hose supports on the roofs of the house and the garage so that he could keep sprinklers running.

Polly: He did all this while hiding from the police and firefighters, who had told everyone to evacuate.

John: It was terrible, at midnight, sneaking into my own house, turning boxes over in the basement and the garage. I rigged the copper pipes twenty feet up, tied to the chimney with duct tape. I set one to cover our roof and our neighbor's house on Tunnel, and one on the garage to cover our neighbor on Alvarado. There were embers flying and igniting little fires all around the perimeter of the yard.

One can imagine John Armstrong as a dervish of driven activity and ingenuity through the surreal night. After setting up the roof sprinklers, he dove into the camping gear stored in a shed in the backyard and pulled out a portable generator.

John: I set up the generator in the backyard and kept the freezer and ice maker going. Then I ran cables over to the neighbor's house and kept their refrigerator going. We had no power or gas for three or four days.

At dawn John Armstrong was making coffee on a camp stove and serving it to the cops and firefighters he had dodged the night before. He invited the officers going off shift to come into the house to use the bathroom.

Situated on the corner of Tunnel Road and Alvarado, the Armstrongs' house was adjacent to the staging activities of firefighters and gas and electric workers, as well as to police heading up Tunnel Road and the stream of emergency vehicles coming down Tunnel from the fire front in Oakland. The house sits on the lower leg of Alvarado Road and therefore was within the line of defense set up by the Berkeley Fire Department five hundred feet farther up Tunnel at the intersection with Bridge Road. The fire came as close as the foliage directly across Tunnel Road and the houses just above theirs on Tunnel.

The Armstrongs' stretch of Alvarado is completely intact, so it is especially shocking to round the bend and come upon the section that was incinerated.

Polly: A week after the fire, Toni Garrett and Gene Farb hosted a potluck at their house on Alvarado for all the neighbors who lost their homes, put on by the people whose houses survived. The people who were burned out said how important it was to them that this part of the neighborhood is still here—that it gives them a sense of familiarity.

The Farbs' house did not burn; the fire stopped right at their yard. Being a survivor in a devastated landscape could be awkward. But for Toni and Gene it deepened their connection with the community. They opened the house to numerous neighborhood gatherings. Their store extended a discount to fire victims, as did others in the area. Although their house survived, the Farbs had experienced the panic of evacuation along with their neighbors on Alvarado and Vicente.

Removed

Families and firefighters who were away from the Bay Area when the fire struck felt a mix of shock and helplessness when they heard the news reports.

Traveling in Thailand, Jourdan Arenson was as remote from the scene of the fire as one could be. It was already the next day, Monday, but a satellite picture on the television news in his Bangkok hotel room brought him home. Arenson was in his hotel bathroom, shaving, when he suddenly peered at the TV and the picture he saw was his family home on Tunnel Road in flames.

Arenson's mother and father, Lu and Charles Arenson, had bought the 1922 Danish Crosswood house twenty-seven years before, and he had lived nearly his whole life in it.

Apparatus Operator Bob Humphrey is usually on the A shift at Station 2. The day of the fire he and his wife Denise were on a driving trip through the Great Basin, towing a camping trailer behind their car.

Bob Humphrey: We had been traveling east across Nevada and pulled into Cedar City, Utah. At that point everything on the car and trailer hit the fan: the U-joint went out, the steering column starting smoking, warning lights flashed on the dashboard, and the trailer got a flat tire. No one was open because it was the first day of hunting season. I was under my car, trying to see the U-joint, and everyone was driving around me with dead deer on their cars.

Finally I found a car parts store that was open. There was a radio going in the back room and I heard, "The Oakland Fire Department estimates that over a thousand homes have burned. This is the worst fire in U.S. history." I was amazed and couldn't believe what I was hearing. I thought maybe they were

Lu and Charles Arenson lived in this 1922 Danish Cross-wood house on Tunnel Road for twenty-seven years before it burned to the ground. Photo courtesy of Lu Arenson.

talking about an Oakland, Utah. But the guy in the store said, "Where have you been?" and told me that it was in California.

I called Station 2 from a pay phone and was relieved to hear that everyone was okay. But then, when I was telling my wife, I got all choked up and started to cry. I had this big feeling of disappointment that I had missed it.

Some time later, when we were out for the evening with another couple, I heard the woman saying to Denise in the back seat, "You're glad Bob wasn't there, aren't you?" I looked in the rearview mirror and saw her nodding yes.

But no one wants to miss something like that. No real firefighter does.

Firefighter/Paramedic Eddie Pennine, also from the A shift at Station 2, was in New England visiting relatives with his wife, Kathleen, and two-year-old Eddie, Jr., on what Pennine calls a "National Lampoon vacation."

Eddie Pennine: Everything that could have gone wrong did. My kid got chicken pox, my sister got pneumonia and had to be hospitalized, we went to a cabin in New Hampshire with our best friends and the wife got sick and we had to leave. While we were back there we got the news that a friend in California had been killed.

Then, when we were with my family in Rhode Island, I was watching the football game on TV—the 'Niners—and the news came that there was a fire in Oakland. I thought it was probably a warehouse or something. Then they interrupted the game and showed all these homes burning and said it was in Berkeley and Oakland.

It was my shift that was on that day. I couldn't believe it. The biggest fire in my career and I miss it. I was pacing back and forth in front of the TV.

My wife says, "Why are you upset? If you were there you know I'd be so worried."

But you just feel that you lost out on this camaraderie. In the East Coast newspapers they had quotes from the firefighters I knew. It was really frustrating.

Then we got calls while we were still on vacation from friends whose homes were burned. I said, "You can live in our house," and some of them did move in with us.

It was just the icing on the cake: chicken pox, death. We were saying, "Now, what else? If there's going to be a bolt of lightening, let's do it today." We had no idea.

We haven't been back East since. We're afraid to go!

The City's Response

The fire hit Berkeley like an assault. When it was over, the city was left with the wounds of damage, disruption, and expense. The scene was of complete devastation—an entire neighborhood was flattened. Electrical wires, power poles, and charred tree branches littered the streets, making passage impossible or dangerous. Water and power were out. The house sites were buried in tons of ash and twisted debris. "I saw Kuwait," muttered one contractor, referring to the damage in the Persian Gulf War. "This is worse." While those displaced by the fire suffered a form of shock, the municipal body mustered departmental forces to deal with the aftermath like white cells clustering to a wound.

People in Need

Within an hour after Berkeley's first alarm, City Manager Mike Brown had called a dozen or so key city officials to the Emergency Operations Center (EOC) he had set up in the police building. The EOC team stayed on duty for the first twenty-four hours, then met every day for the next eight weeks. They huddled to figure out what city services might be needed and to monitor the progress of the fire, then dispersed to the field each day returning to report on their progress. They scrambled to set up and supply an evacuation shelter with the Red Cross in one of the junior high schools. They found local restaurants and markets that would provide free meals and groceries for evacuees and fire workers. Schools were closed and school workers served meals at the shelter and did other relief chores. The public works department sent people to barricade the streets and to begin to assess the damage. There were concerns for public safety because of the electrical wires and hazardous debris filling the streets. "And there was a real possibility the fire could start back up again, if the winds shifted," said Fire Chief Cates. "A day after the fire there were still lots of hot spots."

Two days after the fire, the state Office of Emergency Services ordered a halt on debris clearing until search-and-rescue teams with trained dogs finished looking for bodies. The next day, 150 search-and-rescue volunteers combed the fire area. There were no fire deaths in Berkeley.

Just finding out the exact number and identity of every house that burned down or was damaged was a daunting task. The final count was sixty-two houses destroyed, five houses damaged, two garages destroyed, one garage damaged, one duplex destroyed. One difficulty was determining whether houses lay in Oakland or Berkeley. The city line bisects at least seven properties in the burn area.

PG&E and Pacific Bell crews were clearing tree branches and stringing electric and phone lines within days after the fire. Reconnecting gas lines took longer. The water utility, the East Bay Municipal Utility District, was working the day of the fire to replace meters, cap ruptured lines, and restore service.

The city manager declared a state of emergency for the city early on the evening of the fire. The following day Mayor Loni Hancock held a news conference to announce what had happened in Berkeley. Two days later the federal government declared a state of emergency, qualifying Berkeley for federal assistance.

As the fire danger wound down, the administrative tasks mushroomed. Donations to fire victims flooded City Hall and had to be organized. Systems had to be set up to track the city's extraordinary firefighting and recovery costs and to apply for reimbursement from state and federal disaster funds. "Costs to the city of Berkeley for fire response and recovery have exceeded $2 million with subsequent expenses expected to climb to more than $3 million when we

A temporary sign indicating the Berkeley-Oakland city line was erected after the fire since all familiar landmarks were gone. Photo © 1991 Harold Adler.

include infrastructure damage to public streets, sewers, hillsides, and trees," said Assistant City Manager for Finance Phil Kamlarz. Also, property tax revenues amounting to about $200,000 a year would be lost to the city during the two to three years expected for rebuilding, he said. Months after the fire, Kam-

Pacific Gas & Electric crews were on the scene clearing branches and reconnecting lines within days after the fire and continued reinstalling utilities over the following months. Photo © 1992 Harold Adler.

larz and the fire recovery staff were still negotiating the city's reimbursement with the Federal Emergency Management Administration (FEMA). Mayor Hancock made a personal appeal to FEMA on a trip to Washington, D.C.

Part of the city's emergency response to the fire victims was mental health counseling. Berkeley has one of only two local mental health departments in the state of California, a division of its Health and Human Services Department. In most places mental health is a county function. One of the things the Division of Mental Health is set up to do is to deal with catastrophe. The department had teams at the evacuation center to provide crisis counseling even as the fire raged. The mental health mobile unit, which normally is used to reach homeless people, roamed the fire area with on-the-spot services for survivors returning to their burned-out lots. The mental health experts counseled the firefighters and police about how to deal with distraught fire survivors and with their own experiences in the fire. They held community support meetings and set up a telephone hot line. Within a week, a storefront walk-in center was opened in the Claremont neighborhood offering mental health counseling, as well as referrals to other services and municipal building-permit information.

A Scarred Land

The hillsides, too, were scarred by the fire. Grasses and chaparral were burned, trees blackened. The hills stood exposed and vulnerable to erosion, the vegetation that had anchored the soil gone. Wildfire is known to follow the roots of a plant deep into the ground. The two-thousand-degree inferno created a condition known as hydrophobic soil, which renders the hillsides impermeable to water. The hills above Vicente Canyon had carried a major drainage system, in the form of Vicente Creek and countless erosion gullies, flowing down under Tunnel Road to Temescal Creek, which runs roughly parallel to Chabot Road. Surveys of the burned hills found that the slopes were so altered by the fire that normal runoff channels no longer existed. With the prospect of the rainy season due to follow the fire season, the city's Department of Public Works launched major erosion-control efforts.

Right: Barrier mesh was stretched across the burned hillsides to prevent erosion. Photo by Jane Scherr.

Below: Work crews installed silt fencing in the fire area. Photo by Jane Scherr.

Above: Volunteers filled sandbags as part of the erosion-control effort. Photo by Jane Scherr.

Left: Hydroseeding took place in the first weeks after the fire. Photo by Jane Scherr.

"We considered the threat of significant land and debris slides occurring after the first heavy rain to be very serious," said Berkeley Public Works Director Jordan Rich. "The burned ground was incapable of absorbing water or channeling it in the normal way. The runoff we anticipated from the hillside and Vicente Creek exceeded the capacity of the twenty-four-inch culvert under Tunnel Road."

Within four days of the fire more than one hundred young East Bay California Conservation Corps workers contracted by the city were at work on the hillsides. They were joined by several hundred volunteers from the U.S. Coast Guard.

In two weeks of labor-intensive work the crews hydroseeded, stretched barrier mesh matting on the hillsides, stacked sandbags, and reshaped some of the slopes. They also installed silt fencing and debris racks in the streambed of Vicente Creek paralleling Vicente Road, to prevent chunks of rock and mud from reaching the storm sewer drainage system under Tunnel Road. Preparations were made to channel water runoff down Tunnel Road and divert it to the sewer farther downhill.

The most visible result was from the hydroseeding. Crews sprayed the bare slopes with a "Berkeley" mix of grass seed: barley, rye, fescue, and clover, mixed with a binding agent of cellulous material (wood fiber or shredded newsprint) and suspended in a greenish-colored solution of liquid fertilizer and water. This fluorescent, grayish green "paint" on the hillsides, covered with yellow protective mesh, was the first sign of recovery.

"Hillside stabilization and debris removal were the most pressing needs, from the standpoint of public safety as well as fire recovery," said Public Works Director Rich. "Unstable chimneys, partially burned structures, hazardous materials, and burned trees and branches required immediate removal from the streets and private property in the fire area."

But the city's attempt to exercise a uniform plan for clearing the burned-out lots ran up against the spontaneous efforts of the first homeowners eager to get rebuilding under way. Jeff Grote, whose Vicente Road house had been among the last on that street to burn, was the first to move a truck onto his

Removing hazardous debris from the burned-out lots was an immediate safety need. Photo by Jane Scherr.

property to start clearing away the charred debris. But the city presented him with a "stop work order."

"The chimneys and walls that still stood on the properties presented a real hazard to the public, so there had to be tight restrictions on individual demolition," said Gil Kelley, the planning department's representative on the city's fire recovery team. "Just as we did after the Loma Prieta earthquake in 1989, we surveyed every structure and notified owners if they were unsafe. Some people wanted to keep their chimneys and rebuild around them."

The chimney of Thad and Carol Kusmierski's Maybeck house on Alvarado Road was one of those cases. The massive chimney was a dominant architectural feature and was all that remained of the house. The Kusmierskis received permission to preserve the chimney and braced it with guy wires while they waited to rebuild.

"The city contracted with an engineering firm to demolish the hazardous structures and clear the lots," said Kelley. "The insurance carriers we talked to said the consolidated approach would be fine, especially since it actually lowered the cost per property."

The controversy over whether residents would be allowed to do their own debris removal bounced back and forth between the neighborhood and the city for a while. Eventually the city council passed an ordinance that declared the city's intent to demolish the unsafe structures. If residents wanted to keep their chimneys or carry out the demolition themselves, they could file an appeal and get a use permit. The distinction was made between clearing the lots, which did not require a permit, and demolition, which did.

"The real issue was control," noted Steve Belcher, an administrator hired by the city to oversee fire recovery. "These were people accustomed to having control over every aspect of their lives. Once the city decided they could have the option to contract the work themselves, most decided to have the city do it."

"Everybody was right on the edge of hysteria in the beginning," recalled Polly Armstrong of the first days and weeks after the fire. Her house, on Alvarado Road, is near the fire area. "My neighbor, Jeff Grote, whose house on Vicente Road burned down, called me on a Sunday morning after he got the stop work order. We sat for about six hours at my dining room table, talking about what had happened, what we wanted to happen, how to get a grip. We decided we needed a representative group to deal with the city." It was Polly Armstrong who helped organize the first of a series of public meetings between fire survivors and city officials. She aided the city's effort to identify which houses had burned and to compile an address list of evacuees.

The Fire Recovery Team

"Monday, the day after the fire, I went to work," Armstrong said. "The city manager arranged for a tour of the fire area for my boss, Councilman Fred Collignon, and me, and Alan Goldfarb and Carla Woodworth, the other council members whose districts border the hills. It was the first time I had any real comprehension of what had happened."

Armstrong's job in City Hall, as aide to Collignon, the council member who represents the fire area, placed her in an ideal position to act as liaison between the city and the neighborhood. "You really needed to get people from the neighborhood together as soon as possible—to let the city talk to them," said Armstrong. "But first we had to locate and contact them.

"I worked with the city manager, Mike Brown, and his deputies, Sean Gordon and Vicki Elmer, to put together a list of houses that were gone and to try to reach the people who had evacuated. We mailed announcements and left phone messages about the public meeting, and a local woman made posters that we put up on telephone poles in the fire area.

"We held the meeting on Monday night, eight days after the fire. We had good attendance; Oakland people came as well. There was a great need on everyone's part to get together, to see one another. There was also a need to keep the meeting from dissolving into a screaming match: 'Why didn't you put out the fire on my house?' There is basically a distrust of city government up there. I was very impressed by the efforts of the city manager and Vicki and of Vivian Kahn and Gil Kelley from Zoning and Planning."

That meeting became the first of the neighbors' weekly information-sharing meetings, which they held in the community every Sunday morning for the next six months. The meeting was also the prototype for regular sessions at City Hall between representatives of the neighborhood group and the city's fire recovery staff.

The city's counterpart to Polly Armstrong was Denise Johnston, who came to work to oversee Berkeley's emergency preparedness and response operations just a week after the fire. Johnston had been hired before the fire from a position with the Florida state government and was tying up loose ends with her old job. "When I heard about the fire on the news, I called up Mike Brown and said, 'I'm on my way,'" recalled Johnston. For the first six months Johnston's primary responsibility was meeting with the neighborhood groups and translating their concerns to the city staff.

Vivian Kahn was one of the city planners who worked to put a human face on the building permit process for the fire survivors. "The city recognized the homeowners' loss and the importance of expediting their permits to rebuild," said Kahn. "At the same time, we had to be sure the new houses wouldn't violate the fire safety standards we had identified, such as the need for adequate space between structures and the use of fire-safe materials. The homeowners were very sensitive about not being used as 'guinea pigs' in having stricter measures imposed than they had before."

Together Kahn, Deputy City Attorney Tom Brown, and the planning department's Gil Kelley worked with the neighborhood group to create an emergency ordinance that tried to reconcile the residents' need to start rebuilding with the city's desire to change zoning and code requirements to strengthen fire protection. They set up a "one-stop" permit counter in City Hall to ease burned-out residents through the zoning and building permit process.

Looking back at the city's response to the disaster, City Manager Mike Brown said, "I don't think there was one city department that was not involved with fire recovery: from City Clerk, to Purchasing, to Building and Codes. That everyone pulled together the way they did demonstrates the type of public-spirited city organization we have in Berkeley."

Aftermath: The Fire Survivors

The devastation is still complete, but life has been stirring. Narcissus, snow-drops, and iris have bloomed on schedule with the early February rains. They stand, in snowy banks and tender clumps, around the brick and concrete path-ways leading to nonexistent houses. Ivy has poked its way up among the ruins—even a firestorm couldn't get rid of it. The rains have also brought up bright green grass on the hillsides that slope up behind the house sites—the results of hydroseeding in the first weeks after the fire.

The "houses" have a tended look. Most now have been cleared of debris—ash a yard deep and the remains of appliances, automobiles, concrete, and rebar. Everything salvageable has been carefully husbanded: brick, from walls and garden paths, and firewood, culled from fire-damaged trees, are arranged in neat stacks. Incidental pieces of crockery, now rediscovered in the ash as old friends, teacups and matching saucers that miraculously survived whole in an exploding house, a welded coin collection that might be worth something someday, a pair of charred silver bracelets, still dainty—all are arranged on a foundation wall, as if on an altar, as relics of a family's material history.

"The neighborhood is still there," says Bill McClung, "just without the houses." The absence of walls gives an affable egalitarian spirit to the hillside. As home-owners turn out to tend their property, they are visible on their house spaces instead of concealed behind walls. The natural setting—canyon, foliage, and sweeping view—is brought into stronger relief.

The neighbors on this stretch of Alvarado Road and along Vicente at the intersection where it joins Alvarado had formed a close community. Morton McDonald, who had lived in his Vicente Road house for forty years and on Alvarado Road as a child before that, noted that while the experience of the fire was a binding force, the sense of neighborhood had already been strong. "When my house burned down, three neighbors' keys burned," McDonald said. "We all had keys to each other's houses. We all looked after each other in a very special way." He noted that the neighbors had organized themselves into a disaster squad to learn how to put out fires and give CPR. They jointly had bought the hillside behind their houses to preserve it as open space and were acutely aware of its potential as a fire-spreader.

At the Walrods' property, somehow the wooden fence and garden gate survived. Stepping through the gate, one sees no trace of a house save foundation walls. In the open place, and extending beyond, is a vibrant, thriving garden of perennials, California poppies, and vegetables.

The massive stone fireplace and towering chimney are all that are left of the Kusmierskis' Maybeck house, dominating the burned-out property. The chimney, which tapers up to a towering height, is supported by taut guy wires. It was spared from the city's hazardous chimney abatement program in the fire's aftermath. So ample is this fireplace—emblematic of the vanished house—it could be said that hearth *is* home.

The sudden and total loss of home and neighborhood was a kind of psychic amputation suffered by fire survivors. Disorientation, anger, mourning, annoyance, and, for some, a sense of liberation were experienced to varying degrees by the men, women, and children whose houses burned down on Alvarado, Vicente, Tunnel, and El Camino roads.

Six months after the fire some of these neighbors gathered in Toni Garrett and Gene Farb's living room to talk about their experiences and how the fire had affected them.

Bill McClung described the "peculiar mix of pain, grief, inconvenience, and joy" he felt at the loss of his house and the prospect of building a new one. "I want people to know that if they are feeling positive they should be able to express that as much as they do their sorrow. It's part of the process, like spring following winter. Life is coming back to the neighborhood—the vegetation is coming back, houses are coming back."

McClung is at one end of the scale in his optimism and enthusiasm at the

The massive stone fireplace and towering chimney are all that were left of the Kusmierskis' Maybeck-designed house. Photo © 1991 Harold Adler.

Rituals

"At Christmastime, when our twenty-six-year-old daughter came back to Berkeley from New York City, she and I devised a ritual to say good-bye to the house. The three of us squatted on the floor of our garage (which didn't burn). We lit a votive candle for each room in the house and then each of us spoke about our favorite memories in that room. The Christmases in the living room, the family discussions around the dining table, the thousands of meals cooked in the kitchen, the havens of our bedrooms. When we finished, we had created a circle of candles. Then we divided up the rooms according to our time spent there and our feelings about them. Guess what? I got the kitchen. Then that person said, 'Good-bye room,' and blew out the candle. This ritual eased us into one layer of acceptance—the planning of it felt creative and we participated in it together as a family."

Fredrica Parlett,
formerly of Alvarado Road

chance for a fresh start. That he did not experience a total sense of loss may be attributed to his fondness for the natural elements, which despite the fire remained, including the grassy hill behind his property, where he himself dug the hiking trails. This is the hill McClung and his neighbors jointly purchased to preserve as open space. His close connection with his neighbors remained too. At the gathering at Toni Garrett's, he shared a parable about grieving that had been translated by a local rabbi, Burt Jacobson, whose house also burned: "The truly joyous person is like one whose home has burned down: she feels her sorrow deeply, but then decides to build again, and over every new stone that's laid her heart rejoices."

Jim Troy echoed McClung's sentiment, saying that he sensed "personal growth" in himself resulting from the forced change from his comfortable setting and set behavior patterns. Troy and his wife, Priscilla, and their teenage son had vacated their Vicente Road house, built in 1913 by architect John Hudson Thomas as the carriage house to the mansion on the corner of Vicente and Tunnel Road. The house was saved from total destruction but was damaged enough to necessitate their moving out during repairs. Their temporary quarters were as different from the stately residential neighborhood as one could imagine: a loft in the wholesale produce district of Oakland, adjacent to busy railroad tracks and the deepwater port.

"The experience was positive and negative," said Priscilla Troy. "In some ways it's like a second honeymoon. We're living more simply now and having fun exploring this warehouse district. There are eight trains a day that go by and we have learned to identify each one by its whistle."

Despite the optimism some were able to feel, the loss of home was nevertheless a complex and disturbing experience. The loss of one's house and everything in it meant disintegration of the fabric of daily life. For most, the house was the unifying element, the source of order. Observations about the incidence of mental illness in homeless people note that simply living on the streets for a while can make a person crazy.

"Order means you don't have to do everything at once," observed Bill McClung. "Without the order implicit in the home—its physical presence, routines, the place where the family comes together—people become disoriented."

"There was no sequence," reported John Traugott, a neighbor on Alvarado Road who is a writer and English professor at the University of California. "I couldn't make connections. All the tissues that seemed to connect parts of my brain were dissolved. Every memory, every picture is gone. Every connection that I could think about is gone. I could think about going from room to room, but there aren't any rooms. There's no path from one place to another."

Carl Goetsch reported a similar state of mind. "For three weeks I was in great confusion. I couldn't put things together and find the rope to follow to unravel this mess."

Jim Pretlow, whose house on El Camino Real, on the west side of Tunnel Road, was severely damaged by the fire, said, "It took me a month before I could sit down and read a newspaper; I could not concentrate. My wife, Mary, is the one who kept things together."

Performing the basic transactions of life required the laborious steps of replacing bills, checkbooks, address books, even cookbooks. "Everything had to be reconstructed," said Debbie Lesser. "It took lots of time and lots of energy."

Most of those evacuating left with the clothes on their backs and with almost none of the necessities of daily existence. Armed with Red Cross vouchers and the prospect of insurance reimbursement, fire survivors thronged East Bay department stores in the weeks after the fire, their arms full of bedding, small appliances, toys, and clothes. Many stores gave a discount to survivors, but proving disaster status was not always easy without official Red Cross documentation. "I showed them my driver's license with my address and said, 'It's not there anymore, isn't that good enough?'" said Esther Hirsh.

In the midst of this shock the fire survivors had to cope with being the object of good intentions. The City of Berkeley's health department, churches and synagogues, workplaces, schools, and private therapists offered counseling aimed at the survivors' posttraumatic stress and other adjustment disorders. While many utilized these services, some found the procedures more superficial than substantive.

"I had offers of counseling from every quarter," said John Traugott. "Every institution I'm connected with plus three or four people in City Hall offered me counseling. Even my insurance company sent out five 'clerks turned into psychiatrists.' They ran through the list of symptoms I can expect. They said I would be angry with my wife, angry at people on the street, that my energy would decline and my sexual activity would diminish. When I asked about the money for my insurance settlement, they said, 'That's for another meeting.'"

"I'm a psychiatrist," said Bennett Markel, who lives on the same stretch of Vicente as Sharon Drager, Morton McDonald, the Christophersons, and the Kusmierskis, "and some of these counselors really aggravated me. I don't know where they got their simplistic notions about what we're going through."

"All the counselors have come out of the woodwork," agreed Sharon

Recovery

"People speak of recovery. Recovery from what? You recover from the flu or a broken bone perhaps. That means that after a period of illness and stress, the body returns to its former condition, wherein all systems of this incredibly complex machine are more or less balanced. I can't speak of other losses. As one of the other fire survivors said, the loss of human life is on a completely different scale than the loss of one's home and material possessions, or even the loss of a long-term marriage.

"The fire has opened up new possibilities for me, and in some strange way, even my family will be stronger. As well as our growth as individuals, we are beginning to find new ways to come together. Rather than thinking about recovery, a return to 'normalcy,' I think about growth, expansion, finding what is true for me without external or social props. It is a slow process of tiny steps toward discovery. I cherish the brief moment of joy when a new impression appears—a white egret standing motionless in Lake Merritt, sudden laughter with a friend, a new sound under my fingers on the piano keys. Yet I wonder if I will ever be able to trust again or to feel the world a safe place? Is there a home for me?"

Fredrica Parlett,
formerly of Alvarado Road

Drager. "The one person I found helpful was Rabbi Steve Chester at Temple Sinai in Oakland," she said. "His congregation has thirty-eight families in Berkeley and Oakland who lost their homes in the fire. I commend Rabbi Chester for the way he is dealing with us. He calls me every six weeks or so to see how I am doing, and he's empathetic, concerned, and matter-of-fact."

Drager, a surgeon and mother of two, leads a busy and complicated life. She says she has refused to allow people to impose a sugar-coated version of the fire experience on her. "I have no sense of personal growth," she said, "no feeling of new beginnings. The fire is a black hole in my life, sucking up my psychic energy. For my husband and me, just dealing with putting our lives back together takes all our time and energy. It makes me angry and crazy. People don't understand all the hurdles we have to go through when they ask questions like, 'Well, have you started your rebuilding yet?' as if it's raising the barn or something. Just get some nails and two-by-fours and start pounding away."

Esther Hirsh and Greg Nachtwey felt that their other burned-out neighbors on Alvarado Road were the only friends who could relate to what they were going through. "Other people seemed understanding at first," said Greg. "Then, after a week they wondered why I still needed to take time off from work. Their comprehension of the impact of this on us was very limited, their tolerance was short-lived. They barely wanted to acknowledge the grief. They said, 'Count your blessings, it's a great opportunity to start fresh.' They didn't realize the enormous investment of time it takes to resolve all the practical issues. They would say, 'How's the rebuilding coming?'"

"A lot of people feel if it's not their tragedy it isn't real," agreed Esther. "When your life is reduced to three feet of ash, it's very difficult to have to deal with the everyday demands of work and family on top of the horrendous demands of finding a place to live, replacing the basics, and dealing with the insurance company."

"The advice in the parable about new beginnings makes me feel terrible," said John Traugott, "because it's such a formula. That formulaic approach belies everything we're really feeling: the complication, the sadness, the disintegration of our lives. It doesn't acknowledge how complicated, how incredibly complex my feelings are. I lived in one place for twenty-two years. It was a house that had a lot of grace, beauty, and architectural interest. I loved it. It's the place where my children grew up. It's the place where I worked. I lost a book I had just finished that was on my hard disk on the computer."

The degree of bitterness felt by the fire survivors appeared to be in direct proportion with the status of their insurance claims. For those whose claims settled quickly, attention was on rebuilding and getting on with their lives, and their attitudes were generally positive. But those still negotiating with insurance adjustors were stuck in an emotional and logistical limbo.

"I have no anger," said Traugott, "except at the insurance companies, who are maybe scoundrels. In my experience with them they have done everything they can to delay, obfuscate, and wear you down until you're ready to accept any settlement."

"We can't even look at house plans," said Esther Hirsh while waiting for her insurance claim to be settled, "since we don't know what size house we will be able to build."

"I find myself feeling incredible anger against the human stupidity that let this fire get out of control in the first place and the persistence of stupidity that could allow another fire to happen," said Bennett Markel.

"There was a reservoir of anger many residents felt over the absence of the fire department on our street the day of the fire," Esther added. "I've been working very hard to keep that expression in a productive vein. By getting involved in the neighborhood group that meets with the city on the rebuilding and zoning issues, I felt I could exert some control over a situation I had no control over at all. The group's work with the city has been very good. I've felt gratified with the results."

Toni Garrett, whose surviving house sits at the edge of a row of charred house pads, offered the observation that the spirit of the people in the neighborhood and their personal ties with one another are stronger now. "I'm impressed by our friends who lost their houses," she said, "by the humor they've been able to display each step of the way—the day after, the week after, even at times when it was particularly painful for them. There is a certain beauty in dealing with it because of the feelings that are able to come out." She noted that many of her neighbors have a lot of difficulty expressing the anger they feel over the situation and that it is not always easy for others to hear the anger. "We don't have the structures in our society for dealing with things like this. That's why getting together like this is so positive."

With their neighborhood erased by the firestorm and families dispersed to temporary housing, the survivors were determined to remain a community. Besides attending meetings with city officials, neighbors met every Sunday morning at a community center to thrash out the maze of problems they faced. Deprived of the daily contact of neighborhood life, groups of women began meeting midweek for breakfast. In every burned-out community in the East Bay, "Phoenix Groups" sprang up to provide a locus for mutual support and neighborhood concerns.

"We felt a strong pull to stay connected to the neighborhood," said Debbie Lesser.

"The groups all met for the same reason," said Carol Kusmierski. "We had been a community before. Now we shared the experience of having gone through a terrible thing together."

Together the women of this neighborhood grieved and observed how the fire experience had changed their families' lives. With the physical house gone the unifying patterns of home life were ruptured. Often, in the immediate days and weeks after the fire when families were searching for a house to rent, their teenagers would stay with friends, apart from their parents. For some families, that arrangement became semipermanent.

The women described this as a move toward autonomy appropriate for their age, rather than estrangement. In spite of the dispersal of her two older sons, Shelley Nan found the fire to be an experience that strengthened the bonds of an already close family.

"In the first few months we were concerned with getting our life back together," said Anne Walrod, who has two high-school-age sons. "Since the fire we depend on each other more, but the teenagers are going their separate ways, too."

Although many teenagers had made command decisions during the evacuation, acting more decisively than their parents, they seemed to have more trouble dealing with the aftermath. The mothers reported that their kids were "numb" and unable to focus on school. Berkeley High School and the private high schools in the area started group therapy sessions and offered extra counseling for the students who lost their homes.

The fire, striking in October, disrupted the college application process for some of the high school students. One junior did not take his PSAT test. Another took "incompletes" in all of her classes. Another, however, immediately sat down and wrote all his college applications, using the experience of the fire in his essay.

"The worst thing," said one teenage girl, "was coming to school wearing brand-new clothes. Everyone knew. They wanted to ask about the fire, but they didn't know what to say. I really didn't want to talk about it."

"The worst thing," said her brother, "was not living near my friends anymore. My best friend lived across the street, but his house burned down too. Everyone moved to different areas."

"We had lived here our whole, entire life," added his sister.

The impact on younger children was even more difficult to decipher. Feeling the physical danger they had been in more acutely than the teens, they also were more subject to fantasy. One little girl, on her first visit back to the family's burned-out property, looked at the ashes and charred remains of her house. "If we just dig down in the ashes, we will find our house," she assured her parents.

Children's artwork after the fire contained a wealth of symbols revealing their feelings about house, family, danger, and fire. Sometimes their actions were fraught with symbolism, too, as in the case of the child who dressed herself in black for several months.

Many parents agreed that they were inclined to try to overcompensate for the disruption of the fire. "We overindulged our children," noted Anne Walrod. "We had been on a straight-and-narrow track before the fire, but afterward we felt we were floundering and not accomplishing much."

"Since they needed everything after the fire, it was easy to fall into an anything-you-want attitude," said Debbie Lesser.

The facts—of what was lost and what was saved in the fire—were irreversible. The choice the survivors had left was how to deal with the situation in which they found themselves.

"It's a very liberating feeling to lose everything you own." That statement by Michael Lesser epitomizes a typical male reaction to the fire's toll, although it is by no means confined to men nor is it the feeling of every man who lost his house.

What Lesser is talking about is transformation. "It's a load off your shoulders not to have fifteen suits to worry about. I just bought a couple of pairs of Levis afterward. My feeling was: I'm going to do what I want for the rest

Vagabonds

"My husband and I have chosen to be vagabonds. For the next four months we will travel—across the United States seeing friends, then to England to be with family, and back across the United States, returning to the Bay Area the end of August.

"Our home, a Danish Crosswood style, was built in 1922 by Mrs. Jensen, now in her nineties, who lives in a retirement center in Carmel. She seems to have forgotten all of her subsequent homes and remembers only her Berkeley home. We saw her shortly after the fire and thanked her for letting us live in her home. She said she heard there had been some trouble and hoped everything was all right now. We said yes. We didn't have the heart to tell her it is all gone.

"It was our family home for twenty-seven years. On the Saturday after the fire, some of us who had shared happy moments in the house joined together at the site to remember. We were all very touched by my husband's observations. He reminded us that the home had indeed been lovely but that the happiness and good times we had there were because of all of us, we made it happen, and that we had it in our power to make it happen elsewhere.

"People say to me, 'It's too bad, you lost your history.' But I tell them, 'I haven't lost my history. I only lost the documentation to my history.'"

Lu Arenson,
formerly of Tunnel Road

of my life, and I really didn't care if it didn't please people." Lesser admitted to having been in the thrall of a temporary euphoria but said the exhilaration was replaced by a permanent conviction about how he should live his life. "I will try not to get in a material trap again. It irritates me that the insurance companies are forcing us to replace all of our personal property in order to be reimbursed. I'm a different person now than I was before, and I want to keep material things at a minimum. People will try to take you down from the lofty place you want to be in. When something like this happens you have to work very hard to stay free."

The women felt the losses differently from the men. They grieved for the tangible presence of their houses, they said, feeling a physical loss.

"Women are the ones who have a much stronger sense of place," observed Debbie Lesser. "My mother even mourned long-distance over the loss of our home and the family heirlooms we had. On the other hand, my husband was euphoric for the first few weeks. He said, 'This is the freest I've ever been. I don't have things like a garden to worry about.' Then he started to get angry about the loss of all the efforts he had put into things like the garden."

"I think women were more affected by the loss of things," agreed Karen McClung. "My husband said that this didn't affect him physically, that he is just someone who lost his house. But that isn't true for me. It's a physical loss."

While Morton McDonald said he wished he had the foresight to store his negatives separately from the photographs so the destroyed photos could be reprinted, most of the husbands in the male-female dialogue said they did not suffer the loss of family photos and memorabilia as much as their wives. Losing photographs was especially painful for the women.

Debbie Lesser mourned the loss of her children's baby books, photos, and her own high school yearbooks. To her, these things were more precious than the art objects that had monetary value. "We lost the chance to share the past with the kids," she said. "The best gesture came from my friend Katy, who had moved away. Immediately after the fire she sent me all the pictures she had of our two college-age sons taken at birthday parties when they were little."

"It's the most poignant loss," said Anne Walrod, "because our kids have lost all their history. They won't be able to show their children when they grow up. I'm afraid they won't be able to remember."

Carol Kusmierski agreed, "We lost the record of what beautiful babies these teenagers were. How will their spouses know how they looked? We have to help them remember all those times."

"We should write it down for them," said Karen McClung. "I had this closet where I kept some of their special baby clothes—the little blue tennis shoes they both wore, the little flowered jumpsuit. I never looked at them but I knew the things were there. I thought if I could make a list of the things, then at least I would have that."

The McClung teenagers were philosophical about the losses. "The material things were not that important," said Nicola. "I did save the picture album. Besides that, everything can be replaced."

"What is important is to be thankful for life," said John.

John said he was looking forward to the new house, which he and his sister were helping to design. Nicola observed that they had belongings acquired over the years that the family had felt obligated to keep. "Now we can have exactly what we want in the house."

"The fire erased all the mistakes," said their mother, Karen. "I know in the future I won't buy as much stuff, and I don't collect things like postcards and letters anymore."

The Lesser family also had philosophical insights into the experience. "What had been given away was saved," said Debbie Lesser. "A pair of candlesticks from Israel were in the car because I had taken them to use with my Sunday school class. And there were photographs we had sent to relatives, which they sent back."

Hannah Lesser was proud of her contribution. A few weeks before the fire the little girl had gotten into her mother's wedding outfit to play dress-up. Her mother was angry when Hannah soiled the wedding robe, which was sent to the cleaners, where it resided during the fire. "That's how I saved my mommy's wedding robe," boasted the five-year-old.

Michael Lesser told the story of the family's rabbi presenting him with a new *tallis,* or prayer shawl. To Michael's protests that the new *tallis* was much larger than the one he had lost in the fire, the rabbi replied, "Yes, but you have grown as a person."

The Next Steps

REBUILDING AND LESSONS LEARNED

Rebuilding

The hills are covered now in thick wild grass, bright green and standing two to three feet high, brought up by late winter rains. The California poppy is in bloom, adding an overlay of deep orange dots, interspersed with blue stalks of lupine and low-lying clumps of soft purple clover.

Charred live oaks, their foliage copper-colored from sudden death by fire, mark the canyons as sentinels of the devastation. Green leaves have come back on some, as death and life vie for dominance in the landscape.

The primary sound is birdsong. In the distance, sounds of hammers and saws from scattered construction echo across the empty canyons, having replaced the hum of the bulldozers that earlier cleared away the charred debris. But mostly the cleared lots stand empty, except for the trace of foundations and front steps and driveway stubs going nowhere, suspended between what once was and what is yet to come. Only the birds are building on schedule, determinedly reclaiming the surviving trees and shrubs for nests.

Rebuilding was the task that tested people's endurance, as the fire had tested their courage. Sisyphus's rock could not have felt like more of a burden.

In the beginning, the vision of the neighborhood that once was had hovered wraithlike over the ruins, a persistent image pressed into the mind's eye, after the material stimulus to sight had vanished. People imagined the house that was gone and the community that had dispersed, determined to reconstitute them. But visualizing the new house was harder. For many, worn down by the ordeal of coping with the fire aftermath, the idea of "getting on with life" did not include the laborious steps of selecting architect and builder, or of dealing with the bureaucracy of building permits, or remaining in temporary quarters for the year or more it would take to rebuild. For many it took a year just to settle with their insurance companies.

In that year the bonds with the old neighborhood had loosened. The rebuilt neighborhood was an uncertain prospect. The new houses would be bigger and of different styles than the ones that had burned down. Even the streets would no longer look the same, stripped of the leafy sycamores that had provided shade, character, and grace. An outcry arose when one day soon after the fire the neighbors discovered that tree crews had taken out many fire-damaged trees. "They didn't consult us and they didn't consult an arborist to see if the trees might have survived." The patience to wait for new trees to grow was part of the vision required to endure rebuilding.

For those whose desire to rebuild had been eroded by time, separation from the neighborhood, or an unwillingness to build in a place whose character was as yet unformed, selling the empty lot seemed the best option. Six months after the fire, For Sale signs appeared to outnumber contractors' signs on the burned-out streets. Buying a house in an established neighborhood allowed people to put their uncertainty about rebuilding behind them. Sometimes the decision to sell didn't come until they saw how much their insurance settlement would be. When a woman who had occupied her house for many years received a million dollars from her insurance company, she was flabbergasted. Her modest house had ridden the crest of the California real estate market and provided her with a windfall. But tax laws would not have allowed her to keep her windfall for long. So, not inclined to replace her lost house, she invested in a new one.

The simple assumption that one's insurance would cover the losses of the fire proved to be a naive reading of the complex thicket of insurance and tax policies. First, there was the issue of full replacement. Some long-time residents found they were underinsured, that their coverage had not been increased to match inflation. The concept of "guaranteed replacement"—full replacement regardless of the cost—became the new credo, but unfortunately for many, conversion came after the fact. Others in the area who hadn't lost their homes nervously checked their policies and insisted on adding this coverage. So many burned-out residents found their policies lacking that they began to question why their insurance companies had not encouraged them to upgrade their coverage over the years. Finally, banding together, the neighbors enlisted the political force of the state's new, reform-minded insurance commissioner, John Garamendi, and got their companies to concede full replacement for them whether their policies included the provision or not.

After the issue of coverage, homeowners and insurance companies went head-to-head on the question of requiring the claimant to replace every lost possession in order to receive a full cash settlement. Homeowners protested: "What if I want to build a smaller house?" "What if I don't need three TV sets? I think I should be able to use the insurance money for something else." The Internal Revenue Service got in on this, ruling at first that any difference between settlement amount and replacement expenditures would be subject to capital gains tax. "But I've already been taxed on this money before!" cried the outraged homeowner. "Once when I earned it and once when I spent it." Eventually, through the intercession of their state and federal legislators, the homeowners were recognized as disaster victims rather than as speculators and were relieved of a strict reading of the tax laws.

The process of documenting replacement costs was so technical that homeowners, regardless of whether they planned to rebuild, had to enlist the services of an architect or contractor to help them estimate what their house would cost to replace in every detail.

Glenn Jones, a Berkeley-based contractor whose Oakland hills home is in Claremont Canyon just beyond the reaches of the fire, prepared specification packages for homeowners' insurance claims. "I had the client take a mental walk through the house that was lost in order to describe every element," Jones said. Once the "specs" were complete, he presented them to the insurance adjustors—and suddenly found himself in a new role as negotiator. "Many of the insurance adjustors seemed to have a very cynical attitude toward the homeowners' claims," he said. "Sometimes the settlements that were offered appeared to be based on how little the adjustor thought he or she could get away with. These people who had lost their homes were in a vulnerable state, and needed someone to represent them."

Architect Bennett Christopherson, who lost his Vicente Road house in the fire (the very first house he designed, thirty years before, which he and his wife Arlyn had bought from his original client), saw seven others he designed destroyed in the fire. His Berkeley architectural firm was busy drawing plans for new houses and producing specifications for scores of those that had burned.

"It was necessary to reconstruct every detail to develop a picture of the house that was there," Christopherson said. "In some cases we would have an actual photograph to go from, but it was often a photo sent by a previous owner. One family called up from out of state, offering to send photos when they heard that their old house burned down. So our client would have a photo to present, but with other people's furniture in the picture.

"We ended up making packets for our clients of drawings and specifications of their houses, even when they did not intend to rebuild. We had to be able to tell the insurance company whether the walls were gypsum board or plaster, what size were the moldings, how many panels the doors had.

"A big question was: do you estimate the cost of replacing exactly what was there, even if it included archaic systems and materials, or do you propose a new house, equivalent in quality but with state-of-the-art building techniques, such as insulation, safety glass, and reinforced foundations? People had arguments with their insurance companies over code upgrades, which the companies were not inclined to pay for.

"Our approach was to be very literal-minded on finishes and materials—

insist on the value of the mahogany, for example—but to go with state-of-the-art on the technical side. This often meant negotiation with the insurance company. In one case, when the adjustor turned down our specifications for code upgrades, we came back with a schedule for exact reproduction of all the obsolete systems. Then they found out it would cost a lot more to reproduce the old cord and socket electrical wiring, for example, than to put in grounded outlets according to today's standards."

Tolerance and even affection for the details of construction is what set apart those who pushed ahead with their building plans from those who shrank from the process. "The people who were first on their block to come in for house plans were the adventurous ones," said Christopherson. "They were the ones who thought that building a new house would be just an awful lot of fun.

"They weren't intimidated by the process of choosing thousands of things—the finish on a doorknob, the pattern of tile, or fixtures for the bathroom—that you have to go through when you build a house. Maybe they were people who had built a new house before, or had always wanted to. They are devoting practically full time to it. It's a time commitment on the level of starting a business: you spend thousands of hours. Those who don't have the time are probably buying instead."

Christopherson said that only a few residents planned to duplicate exactly the house that had burned. Most who rebuilt saw the opportunity to have the house they had always wanted. "Everyone wants change," Christopherson said. "Everyone is building larger. They are expressing themselves through new designs. People who had a very modern house are changing to traditional styles, drawing from Craftsman, Tudor, or English cottage. Others want a modern house in the International or Bauhaus mode. A modern design, with a flat roof and stepped-back levels, works well on the hillside lots, and we are seeing some large, beautiful ones.

"People are concerned about fireproof materials. Using tiles in place of a shake roof and stucco instead of wood changes the character of a house.

"Mainly they are looking at design changes that will enhance the way they live. They want convenience features they may not have had in an older house like closets, bigger kitchens, or an entrance into the house from the garage. And in a few of the hillside houses we are putting in shaftways for elevators.

"There's a different way of living than when houses were designed seventy years ago. People had been living with inconvenient floor plans that were not designed for them or for modern life. They were making accommodations.

"In a short period of time, about three months, I talked to a hundred people who lost their houses in the fire. I began to see the patterns of family life, and how people are affected by each other's habits, and had an insight into what is important to people now. The biggest concern is privacy and individual space. They want us to design places for them to go away and be quiet. For example, some had remodeled their old houses and had really swell master bathrooms, with his and hers everything. But they didn't want to reproduce that arrangement. They asked for smaller, separate facilities. People really prefer a little private time."

As house plans were drawn and framing began to appear on the lots, some viewed the new, larger designs with alarm. They did not want to see their neighborhood transformed by oversized, out-of-scale "blockbuster" houses. Rebuilt houses were placed at new angles on their lots in order to maximize views or sunlight, but potentially blocking the views or sunlight of the as-yet-unbuilt house next door.

"Size by itself is not necessarily a negative factor," suggested Christopherson. "It's not what you do, it's how you do it." The architect explained that a well-designed house can present less "bulk" while still having more square feet of area inside. "For example, you can excavate into the hillside to add floor space."

He continued, "Berkeley has a very sensitive system for checking with the neighbors directly across and on either side for zoning approval." A zoning permit addresses the factors of building height, bulk, distance the house is set back from the property line, position on the lot, and placement of windows.

Neighborhood review is a feature of the streamlined zoning permit process the City of Berkeley adopted to deal with the rebuilding needs of the fire survivors. The process was hammered out between the city's planning staff and the burned-out homeowners in the first months after the fire. The planners sought to balance the distraught neighbors' needs for expedited permits with the city's interest in exercising some controls.

The intent of neighborhood review was to allow neighbors to consult each other during the house design stage and situate their houses so that the views and privacy of each are maintained.

"I think Berkeley did the thing right," said Christopherson. "To have more detailed height or setback requirements would work in an infill situation, where an occasional house was being added to an existing neighborhood, or in a single mass development. But this neighborhood is starting from scratch and every homeowner is doing different things at different times. By having to consult each other, the one who builds first is protected from the results of an unknown design going in after it's too late to change his house. And likewise, the neighbor who builds subsequently can review the first house in light of her proposed plans. The neighbors can act together to protect each other's views. In most cases they have."

One Year Later: A New Fire Season

The season has come full circle. The tall grasses on the hillsides have turned brown and dry, a new crop of tinder. The warm, sunny days of early autumn would feel like summer if the equinoctial lengthening of the sun's rays did not give a deeper color to the sky. The ripeness of the season is palpable as the richer light seems swollen by the compression of the day.

There seems to be a building frenzy now. Some houses are completed. Others in stages of excavation or framing. The narrow streets are choked with massive construction machinery that may not even have existed when some of the original houses were built: top-heavy cement mixers, towering cranes and drills, elongated flatbed trucks stacked with board feet of lumber about to be transformed into a home.

"We are building the new classics!" a Vicente Road resident proclaims.

Right: By late summer the seasonal grasses had turned dry again, a new crop of tinder. Photo © 1992 Harold Adler.

Below: The framing of a new house overlooks the burned-out lots on Vicente Canyon. Photo by Ron Delany.

The Berkeley neighborhood is on its way to reestablishing itself as a place to live. By the end of the summer the city is busy processing building permits for the fire area.

The new building goes on against the backdrop of the hills, changing in their natural cycle to the same state they were in when the fire struck.

On the anniversary of the fire, people gather to observe the day and note that the fine autumn weather can never be enjoyed without a trace of apprehension, a glance at the hills. It's fire season again, and although they resolve not to let the same conditions repeat themselves, they wonder how much control anyone has over wind, temperature, and dried-out wild vegetation. They want assurances that the fire department will never allow another conflagration to happen.

Fire Prevention Costs Money

In the postfire year, Berkeley city and fire department officials moved quickly to improve the city's fire safety and fire preparedness capacity. They looked at every element of fire prevention and response over which the city might have control, including existing practices.

The fire officers knew the fire had caught them and the Oakland department by surprise. They knew they needed better weather alerts and fire patrols and more coordination with nearby cities. They knew their fire dispatchers needed literally to be on the same wavelength as the firefighters, as well as to have the same understanding of the city's terrain and department procedures. In its study of the October fire, the California Office of Emergency Services recommended that Berkeley separate the fire dispatch operation from that of the police. The study stressed the need for in-depth training and full-time supervision for fire dispatchers.

Diminished funding over the years had stretched the fire department's resources and deferred the upgrading of thousands of feet of water main to city hydrants.

The conflagration of October 1991 gave tangible evidence of the need to increase public spending for fire protection. The city of Berkeley, like most cities in California, had been caught in a budget squeeze in recent years. Cutbacks from the counties and the state, as a result of the loss of federal programs and a recessionary economy, had forced the city to make tough choices in reducing services.

"At the time of the October fire we were living with severe budget constraints," said Fire Chief Cates.

As the public officials identified all the steps the city should take—stiffening fire-safe building code and zoning requirements, increasing fire inspections, upgrading antique water mains, adding fire patrols and equipment—they realized that the price tag for these measures ranged from nominal expense to millions of dollars. In a period of reduced revenues and a citizenry already feeling overtaxed, the need to finance these programs challenged the ingenuity of the fire department and other city staff. It also challenged the seriousness of the public's demand for increased fire protection.

The people of Berkeley responded to the challenge. In the November 1992 general election, a $55 million, twenty-year bond issue for citywide fire prevention was overwhelmingly passed. The bond revenues will replace 200,000 feet of deteriorated, subsized water mains throughout the city. Subsized water mains—four-inch mains dating from 1911—cannot carry the volume of water needed to meet modern flow requirements. Moreover, over the years, some sections had become clogged with mineral deposits, further reducing their diameter. The bond measure will also pay to install several high-capacity water pumps to bring salt water from the bay to the densely built central part of Berkeley; in the event of disruption of the regular water system in an earthquake, these pumps will provide water for firefighting. The measure also contributes Berkeley's share of funds for a new fire station high in the hills. Construction and staffing costs will be assumed jointly by Berkeley, Oakland, the East Bay Regional Parks District, and possibly the University of California, all of which own contiguous open space land. The station will be outfitted as a major emergency facility for the region, with space for emergency vehicles, supplies, and equipment needed for a major fire or earthquake. The plans even envision a helicopter landing pad on the site.

Berkeley Fire Prevention Today

Eve of the Firestorm

Just five months before the October conflagration, in a prophetic statement, Chief Cates exhorted the city council to enact a ban on any new wood-shake roofs in the hazardous fire area. In his statement to the council the fire chief said:

> The last five years of drought and the past (December 1990) freeze have heightened the concern for another fire disaster in the Berkeley hill area. Combustible wood-shakes and shingles will ignite from very small firebrands, embers, and sparks. They [the shakes] then produce large flaming brands that can be carried a great distance by the wind to ignite other buildings with wood-shakes and shingles. This occurred in the 1923 fire. Firefighters would set up a line of defense on one street as rooftops would ignite several blocks behind them. In a conflagration, it is very difficult for the fire department to provide a line of defense, as the rapid travel of fire causes dilution of fire department resources.

One may ask why such a ban was not already in place, given the proximity of the dry open lands and the intermittent reminder of the threat of fire. Yet, as Cates had observed, it had been nearly seventy years since a fire of conflagration magnitude had struck Berkeley.

The city council passed the fire chief's measure to require the use of the highest grade of fire-retardant roofing on new or replaced roofs in the June before the October fire. In the wake of the fire, Assemblyman Tom Bates, whose district is in the East Bay, pushed through a similar measure in the state legislature. But the effect of those bans will be felt only over time, as new houses are built or old ones reroofed.

The Hazardous Fire Zone

One of the city's first projects after the October fire was to enlarge the area designated as hazardous fire zone and increase the level of fire prevention services to it. Fire Marshal Gary Bard and city planners created a district expanded tenfold to include a wider swath of north Berkeley and all of the hill area in the south, totaling 8,300 properties.

The new zone included the old "hazardous hill area," so called because of its proximity to the Hayward earthquake fault. The fire hazard in the hill zone is exacerbated by the area's narrow, winding streets, which could hamper evacuation and access for emergency vehicles. In a major earthquake, fires starting from broken gas lines would be hard to control because of broken water mains and ruptured streets.

To pay for the additional fire prevention and inspection programs in the fire zone, the city council created a "special assessment district." Property owners were asked to tax themselves at a rate of fifty dollars per year. Residents were given the chance to protest and reject the tax by mailing a protest form to City Hall, but most people supported the measure.

Under the new fire prevention program, residents in the hazardous fire zone are required to keep their property cleared of overgrown grasses and brush in an area thirty feet from the house, to prune back tree limbs hanging over chimneys, and to install spark arrestors on their chimneys. Inspectors will make annual fire-season inspections of every property in the fire zone.

Every neighborhood will have an evacuation plan, which includes using the concrete-stepped footpaths that cut through many hilly blocks. Running straight up and down, the paths were intended originally as a means for hill dwellers to walk directly down to the main north-south streets in the days when streetcars ran, avoiding the longer route on the curving streets around the contours of the hills. "The paths are an ideal safety feature, in that they will allow people to evacuate without having to rely on their cars, which could get stuck if streets become impassable," said Fire Marshal Bard. "But right now many of the stairways are badly overgrown or dilapidated and are unmarked."

Fire inspectors will teach neighborhood groups about fire prevention, evacuation routes, and the need to keep their narrow streets clear for emergency access. "Public education and training are a central part of the fire preparedness plan," said Bard, "because without community support the program won't get very far." The public will be able to enroll in emergency response training classes and learn everything from safe evacuation methods to handling hose lines.

"Spontaneous volunteers were a big part of our effort in fighting the October fire," said Chief Cates. "People want to be prepared to help defend their own neighborhoods, so for the sake of their safety and usefulness, we might as well have them trained."

Weather Alerts

The assessment district also will pay to restore weather alerts and patrols during critical fire weather. All the cities along the park border now have access to a new technology: remote automated weather stations. These stations take automatic readings of temperature, humidity, and wind direction and velocity and send them out to all participating fire departments. At the Berkeley fire headquarters, the acting assistant chief of the day calls up the readings on a computer program and sees them displayed on the screen in graph form.

"This is an updated version of the red-flag alert the forest service has been using for years," said Cates. "It can notify neighboring cities and the county that they could be called for mutual aid." Also, firefighters in the hill zones now carry portable weather kits, which include elaborate thermometers that give temperature and humidity for a specific site.

In critical fire weather, reserve fire crews will come on duty to patrol the hills. "They will be just like sentries," said Cates, "marching back and forth

The cities of Berkeley and Oakland signed a new "automatic aid" agreement for joint fire response. Here (from left to right), Oakland Mayor Elihu Harris signs, as Berkeley Mayor Loni Hancock, Berkeley Fire Chief Gary L. Cates, and Berkeley City Councilman Alan Goldfarb look on. Photo by Jane Scherr.

along the fence line, with observation points to stop and look around. Depending on the severity of the weather conditions we would send one, two, or three patrols. If there is a fire, the engines on patrol would be part of the response."

Automatic Aid

Recognizing the need for a much more systematic approach to mutual aid in the event of another potentially catastrophic fire, the Berkeley Fire Department inaugurated new "automatic aid" agreements with the Oakland Fire Department and with each of the other surrounding cities, as well as with the fire departments of the parks district and the Lawrence Berkeley Laboratory. The new plan, drafted and negotiated by Assistant Chief Paul Burastero, will be a blueprint for other automatic aid agreements in the future. Under the

plan, the fire companies of bordering jurisdictions automatically come to fires that occur in the "mutual response areas" of each city. The participating fire jurisdictions now hold joint training exercises, including one each spring before the start of the fire season. To assure coordinated communications, one radio channel has been dedicated for use by all the fire departments involved in a fire, with dispatchers in each city monitoring that channel.

The Dispatch Center

The disaster of the East Bay fire generated a critical look at the communications center. Recommendations for change came from the state Office of Emergency Services (OES). The OES strongly suggested separating the police and fire functions and reinstituting vigorous training in fire practices. A fire department study noted that the current brief training period allows only a sketchy understanding of fire procedures and requires no knowledge of Berkeley streets or neighborhoods, which was an essential element in evaluating the emergency calls that came in on October 20.

Fuel Management

Berkeley's fuel management program, started after the Wildcat Canyon fire of 1980, calls for well-cropped fuel breaks and vigorous enforcement of the residential hazardous fire zone. The premise is that a fire starting in the wildlands can be stopped before it burns down into the populated area and does extensive damage.

"The expectation is that a fire starting in the park can be stopped at the crest of the hill," said Captain Orth, one of the engineers of the original program. "That assumption is based on what we know about 1923, the pattern of the winds, and how we fought the Wildcat Canyon fire of 1980."

Conclusion

The ongoing anxiety over wildfire in the hills affects hill residents and fire-fighters alike. Neither want to find themselves in the path of another October firestorm, fighting it or fleeing from it. Citizens believe that their civic institutions, including fire departments, should protect them. Firefighters ask for public support for fire prevention programs. Those programs are the instrument of reconciliation between the two. Governments, by enacting the measures, and the public, by following them, both assume some responsibility for fire protection.

But the hill dwellers' primal question, "Are we safe?" never can be answered in the absolute. "There is a risk to living in the hills," say the fire professionals. "People have to assume some responsibility for where they choose to live."

That responsibility goes beyond keeping brush cleared and replacing shake roofs. It means having a plan for evacuation from a fire that may be inevitable. It involves an exercise of judgment when choosing the location of one's house. Does the fact that a city has allowed a subdivision to be carved out of a brushy canyon or has approved high-density building on narrow, winding streets automatically give a stamp of safety to those neighborhoods? In the future, the public will insist that policymakers share the responsibility by making fire safety one of the conditions of building approvals. Too often in California, the issues of development are framed in narrow economic terms—the promise of increased tax revenues or developers' fees—at the expense of a bigger picture that includes the forces of nature.

The superimposed structures of human civilization—cities and suburbs, power plants and freeways, cultivated fields and factories, aqueducts and dams—can obscure but not erase the natural forces that shape the state. Too much rain, too little rain, mudslide, fire, and earthquake constitute the backdrop against which the built culture exists.

"If I worried about earthquakes, I'd live in Kansas!" shrugs the veteran Californian. Meanwhile, the Kansan is concerned with tornados.

Yet there must be a middle ground between fatalism and flight in deciding how and where one lives. A thoughtful approach that respects the tremendous forces of nature is as important as environmental policy that respects nature's fragility. Both are grounded in the concept that human life exists as part of the natural system and will affect and be affected by it.

The burnt hills of Berkeley and Oakland may well become the new models of mutual coexistence with nature for the rest of the state's wildland-urban intermix.

"Windows of conflagration"—in which hot, dry winds blow out of the northeast, lowering the humidity and raising the temperature—will continue to occur. Houses in the rustic hill areas will continue to be built. But the new

Gardens of drought-tolerant and fire-resistant California native plants have become symbols of the rebirth of the fire communities. Photo © 1992 Harold Adler.

versions of Red Riding Hood's cottage will not be shrouded in woods, and their roofs will be fire-safe.

The managers of public land—cities, the Regional Parks District, the University of California, and the California Department of Forestry—will coordinate their "fuel management" efforts and keep flammable grasses, brush, and trees cut back. The public entities will realize that their responsibilities, and their vulnerability to fire's spread, do not stop at their own borders and will share information, resources, and emergency response activities.

Cities will require fire-safe building practices of new houses. They will figure out ways to make narrow streets wider: either by easements through private property or by severe restrictions on parking. They will be forced by the public to consider access and fire safety before they approve new housing developments in the wildland-urban intermix.

Some of the lots on which people decide not to rebuild will be dedicated as public open space, purchased for that purpose by nonprofit agencies.

People who are replanting their gardens will look to the California native species, which are both drought-tolerant and fire-resistant. Plants, cultivated and wild, were the first signs of life to reappear after the fire. And gardens, planted communally and on private plots, have become symbols of the new life of the fire communities, risen phoenix-like from the ashes. They have also become manifestos of a new way of planting, building, and dwelling in the fragile, fire-prone, and beautiful East Bay hills.

Appendix

BERKELEY FIRE DEPARTMENT

These are the Berkeley Fire Department members who took part in fighting the October 20, 1991, conflagration. They are grouped by rank within each geographic location. Because of the duration of the fire, most fire personnel served in a number of areas. This list shows each person's initial assignment.

Vicente Road area
Lieutenant Arthur Wolf
Apparatus Operator John Frankel
Apparatus Operator Jarrel Jung
Firefighter Mark Caldwell
Firefighter Brian Corrigan
Firefighter Richard Ellison
Firefighter Fred Gomez
Firefighter/Paramedic Kurt Chun
Firefighter/Paramedic Robert Smith
Firefighter/Paramedic Thomas McGuire
Firefighter/Paramedic Mark Mestrovich

Roble Road area
Lieutenant John Anderson
Lieutenant Neil Lochhead
Lieutenant Charles Miller
Lieutenant Debra Pryor
Lieutenant Kevin Revilla
Apparatus Operator George Fisher
Apparatus Operator Rick Guzman
Apparatus Operator Gorman Lau
Apparatus Operator Randall Olson
Apparatus Operator Wayne Lynch
Apparatus Operator Douglas Schultz

Apparatus Operator Brian Ward
Apparatus Operator William Wigmore
Firefighter Bruce Johnson
Firefighter Fred Ogleton
Firefighter Harry Vernon
Firefighter Paul Wilson
Firefighter/Paramedic Guy Gash

El Camino Real area
Lieutenant Michael Nagamoto
Lieutenant Gene Smith
Lieutenant Avery Webb
Apparatus Operator Gene DeWindt

Apparatus Operator Kim
  Larsen
Firefighter Walter Fielding
Firefighter Dennis Foley
Firefighter Charles Morris
Firefighter/Paramedic Gilbert
  Dong

Tunnel Road area
Captain David Orth
Captain Earnest Jones
Lieutenant David Allen
Lieutenant Richard Assoni
Apparatus Operator Hurey
  Clark
Apparatus Operator Stanley
  Dugar
Apparatus Operator John
  Higgins
Apparatus Operator Bill
  Meilandt
Apparatus Operator Harvey
  Robinson
Apparatus Operator Ken Vallier
Firefighter Ace Adams
Firefighter Rodney Foster
Firefighter George Huajardo
Firefighter Shepard Lewis
Firefighter/Paramedic Roxanne
  Jacobs-Carpenter
Firefighter/Paramedic Bill
  Kehoe

Firefighter/Paramedic Ann
  Margaret Moyer
Firefighter/Paramedic Anthony
  Nunes
Firefighter/Paramedic Robert
  Perez
Firefighter/Paramedic Luis
  Ponce
Firefighter/Paramedic Robert
  Young

Alvarado Road area
Captain Ronald Falstad
Captain Robert Steele
Lieutenant Charles Chinn
Lieutenant Richard Schmidt
Apparatus Operator Michael
  Flynn
Apparatus Operator Malcolm
  Greene
Apparatus Operator John
  Hawkins
Apparatus Operator Tao
  Takaoka
Apparatus Operator Stanley
  Zukowski
Firefighter Jerry Franks
Firefighter Daniel Galaviz
Firefighter Jeffrey Johnson
Firefighter Joseph Kokx
Firefighter Norman Kreiss
Firefighter Lester Putnam

Firefighter Michael Staples
Firefighter/Paramedic William
  Billau
Firefighter/Paramedic Karen
  Parroff
Firefighter/Paramedic John
  Mason
Firefighter/Paramedic Kathy
  Voelker
Firefighter/Paramedic Dion
  Williams

**Assigned to cover the rest of
the city during fire**

Engine No. 13
Lieutenant Dennis Gray
Apparatus Operator James
  Austin
Firefighter Bill Rodgers

Paramedic Ambulance P-114
Firefighter/Paramedic Mike
  Gonzales
Firefighter/Paramedic Melora
  Valentine
Firefighter/Paramedic Sam
  Hoffman
Firefighter/Paramedic Donna
  McCracken

Support functions
Captain Curtis Colagross
Captain Ronald Littley
Captain John O'Reilly
Captain Christopher Pinto
Lieutenant Craig Green
Lieutenant Myles Meier
Lieutenant Lucky Thomas
Lieutenant Richard Watters
Apparatus Operator James
　Carter

Apparatus Operator Michael
　Posadas
Inspector Wayne Inouye
Inspector Jonathan Hunt
Inspector David Ross
Firefighter/Paramedic Warren
　Davis
Firefighter/Paramedic Aaron
　Lee

Command staff
Chief of Department Gary L.
　Cates
Deputy Chief Billy P. White
Deputy Chief Daniel T. Salter
Assistant Chief Gary W. Bard
Assistant Chief Melvin
　Thompson
Assistant Chief Paul Burastero
Assistant Chief David Leimone
Captain Wayne Dismuke

STATEWIDE FIRE DEPARTMENTS

Fire companies from counties throughout northern California responded to statewide calls for aid.

Alameda County
Albany Fire Department
Castro Valley Fire Prevention
　District
Dougherty Regional Fire
　Authority
Eden Consolidated Fire
　Prevention District
Emeryville Fire Department
Fairview Fire Prevention
　District
Fremont Fire Department

Hayward Fire Department
Lawrence Livermore Labora-
　tory Fire Department
Livermore Fire Department
Newark Fire Department
Pleasanton Fire Department
San Leandro Fire Department

Calaveras County
Calaveras Consolidated Fire
　District

Contra Costa County
Contra Costa County Fire
　Department
Crocket-Carquinez Fire
　Prevention District
Richmond Fire Department
Riverview Fire Prevention
　District

El Dorado County
Latrobe Fire Prevention District

Fresno County
Fresno Fire Department
Mid-Valley Fire Prevention
  District
North Central Fire Prevention
  District

Glenn County
Artois Fire Prevention District
Hamilton City Fire Department
Kanawha Fire Prevention
  District
Willows Rural Fire Prevention
  District

Marin County
Alto Richardson Bay Fire
  Prevention District
Kentfield Fire Prevention
  District
Marin Consolidated Fire
  Department
Mill Valley Fire Department
Novato Fire Prevention District
San Rafael Fire Department
Tiburon Fire Department

Mono County
Mammoth Lakes Fire
  Prevention District

Placer County
Newcastle Fire Prevention
  District
Penryn Fire Prevention District
Placer Foothills Consolidated
  Fire Prevention District
Placer Hills Fire Prevention
  District
South Placer Fire Prevention
  District

Plumas County
Quincy Fire Prevention District

Sacramento County
American River Fire Prevention
  District
Folsom Fire Department
Galt Fire Department
Sacramento Consolidated Fire
  Prevention District
Sacramento Fire Department

San Francisco County
San Francisco Fire Department

San Joaquin County
Clements Rural Fire Prevention
  District
Delta Fire Prevention District
Liberty Rural Fire Prevention
  District
Stockton Fire Department

Tracy Fire Department
Waterloo-Morada Fire
  Prevention District
Woodbridge Fire Prevention
  District

San Mateo County
Colma Fire Prevention District
Daly City Fire Department
Menlo Park Fire Prevention
  District
Pacifica Fire Department
Redwood City Fire Department
San Bruno Fire Department
South County Fire Authority
South San Francisco Fire
  Department
Woodside Fire Prevention
  District

Santa Clara County
Mountain View Fire
  Department
Naval Air Station Fire
  Department
San Jose Fire Department
Santa Clara Fire Department
United Technical Center

Solano County
Dixon Consolidated Fire
  Prevention District

Fairfield Department of Public
Safety
Rio Vista Fire Department
Suisun City Fire Department
Vacaville Fire Department
Vacaville Fire Prevention
District
Vallejo Fire Department

Sonoma County
Bellevue Fire Prevention
District
Healdsburg Fire Department
Rincon Valley Fire Prevention
District

Santa Rosa Fire Department
Windsor Fire Prevention
District

Stanislaus County
Oakdale Fire Department
Oakdale Fire Prevention
District
West Stanislaus Fire Prevention
District

Sutter County
Sutter Consolidated Fire
District
Sutter Fire Department

Tehama County
Tehama Consolidated Fire
District

Tuolumne County
Sonora Fire Department

Yolo County
Willow Oak Fire Prevention
District
Winters Fire Department
Woodland Fire Department

ABOUT THE AUTHOR

Margaret Sullivan is a journalist whose freelance articles have appeared in local, national, and international newspapers and wire services. She also was a general assignment reporter for a small-town weekly newspaper, the *Pacifica Tribune.* Sullivan is intensely interested in political and community issues. She served as the public information officer for the mayor's office in Berkeley and has advised on community outreach and public relations for numerous government entities and nonprofit organizations. While researching *Firestorm!* she worked with those responsible for Berkeley's fire recovery program, gaining unique access to information about the East Bay hills fire from people who lived through it. Sullivan is a Berkeley resident.